KW-305-332

Table of Contents

Appendix 1

NEVER A GOLDEN AGE: AN HISTORICAL PERSPECTIVE

1. Local taxation has existed in England at least since 1250, and central government grants to local authorities since 1835. The share of central government grants in the combined total of grants and local taxes rose from 9.4% in 1879/80 to 65.3% in 1974/75[1]. The proportion of local expenditure raised by locally determined taxes is now less than 20%, after increasing in the 1980s to more than 50% in response to repeated reductions in government grants.

2. During the last 150 years there have been many variations in the system for paying for local services. For example, between 1888 and 1927 a system of assigned revenues was in force in respect of some excise taxes and probate duties. This replaced many previous specific grants. It was proposed to distribute this on a needs basis, using indoor pauperism as the indicator, but the method was rejected because many authorities gave poor relief outside the workhouse. In the words of Foster and others[1]:

> *'This problem of finding the correct acceptable indicator of needs has bedevilled block grant distribution ever since. Sooner or later all the needs formulae evoked a tension which led to their demise. Even the most successful one, the 1958 formula slightly modified in 1966, only lasted for about fifteen years.'*

3. Assigned revenues were abolished in 1929 as part of a wider reform in which the Treasury also succeeded in replacing many percentage grants, paid on a basis which matched a proportion of local authority spending on a service, with grants based on a formula allowing for local resources and needs. Several major reports had analysed in detail the principles which might enable grant systems to achieve equalisation. For example, in a minority report to the 1901 Royal Commission Lord Balfour put forward a system based on equalising resources and needs to enable a standard rate to be levied everywhere in respect of a standard level of service. This scheme has been described as 'very similar to the block grant which was introduced in 1981/82 in England and Wales'[2].

4. The 1929 system used a formula which was particularly obscure in its operation, and was not very successful in terms of equalising resources and needs. In a 1937 book[3], Mabel Newcomer quoted an unnamed official who had been involved in recommending the formula as explaining

---

1   *C.D.Foster, R.Jackman and M.Pearlman: Local Government Finance in a Unitary State (Allen & Unwin, 1980)*

2   *T.Travers: The Politics of Local Government Finance (Allen & Unwin, 1986)*

3   *Central and Local Finance in Germany and England, quoted in Foster and others, Local Government Finance in a Unitary State*

that 'cumulative weighting was carried this far and no further because they knew what results they wanted and this gave just those results'.

5. Since 1945 there have continued to be many radical changes in systems of grant, for example:

— in 1948, resource equalisation for the more disadvantaged half of LAs was achieved by using central government as an extra ratepayer;

— in 1958, local discretion was increased by substituting an unhypothecated block grant for many previous specific grants, although the main purpose of this reform, as in 1929, was to limit the open ended commitment created for central government by a wide range of specific grants based on a percentage of actual expenditure;

— the domestic element of the Rate Support Grant was introduced in 1967 to keep down rates paid by all householders, following the introduction of rate rebates to benefit poor rate-payers in 1966;

— after the 1974 reorganisation, a system of multiple weighted regression analysis was used to distribute the needs element of the Rate Support Grant. This reflected actual spending, and was justified in the 1977 Green Paper which gave the then government's response to the Layfield Report:

'(Existing expenditure is used) because it represents the combined influence of the Government's policies acting through legislation control and advice on particular services and of the policies of individual local authorities expressed in their budgeting and expenditure decisions[1].'

However, it was perceived as helping high spenders more than low spenders;

— in 1981, Block Grant replaced the needs and resources elements. Needs were calculated by Grant Related Expenditure Assessments (GREs) which were intended to substitute an objective assessment of needs for the previous system based on past expenditure;

— rate capping was introduced in 1984, first for selected authorities, followed by powers to cap all councils. This reflected political pressures and an electoral mandate, but went against a previous Government's Green Paper of 1971[2] which said:

'In some countries… a limit is imposed on the rate at which a particular tax can be levied by local authorities, but this generally leads to all levying up to the limit. The tax then ceases to be locally variable and becomes a variant of government grant.'

1   Local Government Finance, Cmnd 6813, 1977

2   The Future Shape of Local Government Finance, Cmnd 4741, 1971

— in 1990, domestic rates were abolished, non-domestic rates were brought under central government control, and Community Charge was introduced. SSAs replaced GREs as the basis for setting needs and grant;

— 1993 saw the abolition of Community Charge and its replacement by Council Tax.

6. Foster and others have shown that between 1883 and 1975, local current expenditure (mainly local government expenditure) rose on average by 3% for every 1% increase in gross national product. Rates were relatively stable at 2% to 2.5% of personal disposable income between 1938 and 1975. The proportion of local expenditure met by central government grants increased to meet the balance of extra cost, from less than 50% in the 1930s to 66% in 1975.

7. After 1976, central government sought to stop the growth in local current expenditure. Imperfections in the grant system which were tolerable for local authorities in a period of growth became more controversial when accompanied by overall cuts or stagnation in spending. Efforts by central government to force cuts in spending by cutting grant levels led to an increase in rates as a proportion of personal disposable income from 2.17% in 1974/75 to 3% in 1984/85, significantly above the long-term historical relationship[1]. As a result of government policies to cut expenditure by reducing grants, the share of local expenditure borne by central grant fell from 66% in 1976 to less than 50% in the 1980s. Since the centralisation of non-domestic rates and the decision in 1991 to increase VAT in order to reduce Community Charge, central government decisions fix more than 80% of local government income.

---

1   *1974/75: Foster and others, Local Government Finance in a Unitary State,1980*
1984/85: Paying for Local Government, Cmnd 9714, 1986

Appendix 2

TRACING THE STEPS – HOW SSAs ARE DERIVED

METHODOLOGY

1. A number of general principles guide assessments. An appropriate client group is identified which as far as possible represents the recipients of the service. This is multiplied by an appropriate unit cost and, for certain authorities, an area cost adjustment (principally to allow for higher labour costs in London and the South East) to determine the assessment:

SERVICE SSA = CLIENT GROUP x UNIT COST x AREA COST ADJUSTMENT

2. The clearest example of a client group is in Education where, for example, school-children resident in the LA's area between the ages of 5 and 11 are the client group for Primary Education. In most cases, however, the client group is not so obvious and a wider group of potential service recipients has been chosen e.g. the population under 5 years of age for Nursery Education. In the Other Services assessments, which are aggregates of a number of different services, there is no obvious choice, and population (enhanced by commuters and visitors) is used. For some assessments, the client group is estimated from selected indicators in the same way as unit costs e.g. Children at Risk, the client group for the Children's PSS assessment.

3. SSAs acknowledge that unit costs can vary between LAs. The research process behind SSAs therefore attempted to identify relationships which accounted for systematic variations in unit cost levels. A set of guide-lines, enshrining the lessons from earlier assessment work, strongly influenced the choice of indicator variables and the nature of the relationships (Box A2.A, overleaf). Relationships were to be built up from indicator variables which might be expected to influence spending and which could not be manipulated by LAs for unfair advantage. There were also a number of principles guiding the use of regression analysis e.g. weightings derived from statistical analysis should be subject to tests of plausibility; statistical significance alone was not sufficient.

EXAMPLE: DERIVATION OF THE CHILDREN'S PERSONAL SOCIAL SERVICES SSA

4. The Children's PSS SSA, being one of the more complicated assessments, illustrates most of the important features of deriving assessments. It includes provision for residential, foster and nursery care; services provided for mentally and physically handicapped children; and relevant social work and administration costs.

5. DoE commissioned the Personal Social Services Research Unit (PSSRU) at Kent University to advise on the formulation of the assessment. In order to avoid the policies of individual LAs from distorting the results, the work matched random samples of children entering care in each authority with similar samples of children not in care, and attempted to identify factors which distinguished the groups. It identified four factors (households which received

GENERAL PRINCIPLES IN DEVELOPING ASSESSMENTS

1. Assessments to be, where possible, the product of the relevant client group and an LA-specific unit cost, allowing separate selection and weighting of appropriate indicators.

2. Basic assessments not to be reworked annually (to promote stability).

3. Where regression analysis used to derive relationships:

    — Indiscriminate use of step-wise regression and highly correlated explanatory variables (as happened in the 1970s) to be avoided;

    — Indicators to be selected on the grounds of plausibility, excluding those which can be influenced by LA policy choices;

    — City of London and the Isles of Scilly not to be used in the analysis;

    — A variety of methods to be used to confirm the plausibility of the indicator weightings, including professional judgement, consensus and other research evidence, in addition to statistical significance.

Supplementary Benefit, had a lone parent, and lived in rented or overcrowded accommodation) which increased the probability of a child being taken into care. The resulting regression formula was not used; instead, DoE used the factors identified by PSSRU to regress against the proportion of children in each LA actually in residential or foster care. Overcrowding was dropped from the relationship because it 'added little to the explanatory power of the equation and its regression coefficient was negative'[1]. The resulting equation explained 73% of the variance.

6. PSSRU also looked at unit costs but did not identify any specific factors as the most important. DoE therefore created a composite indicator (the Children's Social Index (CSI)) composed of several factors thought to be relevant to social disadvantage in children. Composite indicators avoid the problem of unstable regression coefficients which arises when a number of correlated variables are used. DoE state that the construction of the CSI variable was based on advice in a research report by Professor Bartholomew of the London School of Economics (LSE), who was commissioned to provide guide-lines for the construction of indicators of social disadvantage. A relationship was found by regression which explained 41% of the variance in average net expenditure per child in care for the financial year 1987/88.

7. The area cost adjustment is similar for all assessments, and is calculated by applying the proportion of the assessment assumed to cover wage and salary costs by an employment cost adjustment for the area in question. This is derived from data from the New Earnings Survey, an annual 1% random sample of employees, which is used to calculate occupationally-standardised wage rates for each London borough and South Eastern county, and hence for three groups of districts (inner fringe, outer fringe and the remainder).

8. The resulting relationship implies very different SSAs for different types of authority. Areas such as Inner London with a high degree of social deprivation exhibit both high numbers of children at risk and high unit costs, so that total cost differentials per child in the population vary across authorities by a factor in excess of 10 (Exhibit A2.1).

---

1   *Standard Spending Assessments: Background and Underlying Methodology, Department of the Environment, 1990.*

Exhibit A2.1
CALCULATION OF THE CHILDREN'S PSS SSA
Total cost differentials per child vary.

	Oxfordshire	Lambeth		Weight		Oxfordshire	Lambeth		Ratio Lambeth/ Oxfordshire
CHILDREN AT RISK									
Children of lone parents	10.9%	30.9%	x	25.1%	=	2.7%	7.8%		
Children of claimants	7.2%	42.3%	x	7.7%	=	0.6%	3.3%		
Children in rented accommodation	38.8%	72.2%	x	2.5%	=	1.0%	1.8%		
				Less 1%	=	-1.0%	-1.0%		
Children at risk (% of population 0-17)					=	3.2%	11.8%		
UNIT COSTS									
Children of lone parents	10.9%	30.9%		normalised	=	-0.61	4.87		
Annual population decline (1980-1990)	0.0%	0.9%		normalised	=	-0.43	3.61		
People in non self-contained accommodation	0.7%	5.5%		normalised	=	-0.11	3.81		
Children where household head born in New Commonwealth/Pakistan	3.3%	36.3%		normalised	=	-0.43	3.23		
Ward weighted density x 10	17.1	89.9		normalised	=	-0.63	3.26		
Children's Social Index						-2.22	18.78		
multiply by ...					x	182.22	182.22	£	
and add ...						-404.31	3422.07	£	
Basic unit cost						2860.80	2860.80	£	
						2456.49	6282.87		
Multiply by area cost adjustment					x	1.05	1.20	£	
Unit cost/child at risk						2577.35	7510.38	£	2.9
									x
Multiply by % children at risk					x	3.2%	11.8%		3.6
Unit cost/child 0-17						83.75	888.09	£	10.6
Multiply by population 0-17					x	140,166	53,858		
SSA for Children's PSS						11.739	47.831	£m	

DERIVATION OF OTHER ASSESSMENTS

9. Each assessment has its own approach, brief details of which are contained in Table A2.1. Most assessments are based in some way on regressions of actual LA activity levels or actual unit costs, or, where no relationship can be identified, on national averages. The Police SSA is unusual in that it depends solely on officer establishments approved by the Home Office. A few assessments, such as Flood Defence and Coast Protection, are based on actual expenditure in the previous year, because the LA is deemed to have very little control over spending levels.

UPDATING THE ASSESSMENTS

10. DoE's original intention was to keep the methodology the same for a number of years to promote stability. In practice a few minor amendments are usually made each year to respond to criticisms e.g. the revenue interest receipts control total is now split by authority type prior to allocation; the proportion of Education SSA distributed according to Additional Educational Need (AEN) has been reduced for two of the sub-blocks; and the weighting on overnight visitors in the calculation of enhanced population in the Other Services block has been doubled. Other changes have been forced upon the system by external events e.g. structural maintenance of key principal roads has been transferred to capital. But for the most part, SSAs have stayed as originally devised, apart from being increased in line with control totals.

11. Annual discussions on changes in the methodology are conducted within the SSA sub-group (SSASG) of the Settlement Working Group (SWG), which produces a joint report to the Consultative Council on Local Government Finance (CCLGF) in September each year. SSASG consists of representatives of the Local Authority Associations, the DoE and other government departments and meets every 3 to 4 weeks from February to August. All parties make suggestions about the work programme and submit papers for consideration, but the bulk of the research effort (38 out of 54 papers in the 1992/93 round) is provided by DoE. The process is effectively controlled by DoE, which sets the agenda and chairs the meetings.

Table A2.1
SUMMARY OF METHODOLOGIES
The different assessments use several different approaches. All assessments are subject to area cost adjustments relevant to the particular service.

Main Block	Sub-block	Method Used
Education	Primary	The client group is pupils aged 5-10. Unit costs vary according to indicators of Additional Educational Need (AEN), sparsity and free school meals. The weights (20%, 2.4%, 1.2% respectively) were set by judgement, supported by regression analysis in the case of AEN, which is a composite indicator of social deprivation and ethnicity, whose component factor weights were also influenced by regression.
	Secondary	Similar to Primary Education. Client group is pupils aged 11-15.
	Post-16	Similar, except that there is no free school meals allowance and the client group is estimated via an average of students on various courses, weighted according to relative costs. The special needs element (4%) is distributed via pupils aged 11-15 .
	Under 5	The client group is the resident population aged 0-4. 50% of the SSA is allocated via the Additional Educational Needs indicator (AEN).
	Other Education	Similar, except that the client group is the population aged 11+ .
Personal Social Services	Children	The client group is *Estimated Children At Risk*, based on a regression of actual numbers of children in care with indicators suggested by University of Kent research. Unit costs are derived from a regression of average actual expenditure against a deprivation index, the *Children's Social Index*.
	Elderly (Residential)	The client group is based on a regression of the actual proportion of elderly in supported accommodation against the proportions living alone, claiming Income Support and resident in independent homes (in line with research by the Univ. of York). The relevant elderly population is age-weighted. No satisfactory relationships were identified for unit costs, so a national average expenditure less average LA income/head is used.
	Elderly (Domiciliary)	A client group based on a regression of the *cost* of domiciliary care at the level of the individual against various indicators of need in the elderly population. A national average expenditure less average LA income/head is used to determine the unit cost.
	Other Social Services	The client group is the resident population aged 18-64. Unit costs are based on a regression of actual cost/head against the *All Ages Social Index* (AASI), a composite index of deprivation.

Main Block	Sub-block	Method Used
Police		The assessment is based on police establishments approved by the Home Secretary, because these are not within a LA's control and labour costs are the most significant element of the budget.
		The unit cost is a national average (subject to area cost adjustment), set so that SSA matches the required control total.
Fire & Civil Defence		The client group is the resident population. Unit costs are based on a regression of actual cost/head with the number of fire and false alarm calls, the ward-weighted density and the hectares defined as 'A' risk.
Highway Maintenance		The 'client group' is road length, weighted according to type of road to reflect historic relative costs (now split by Primary Route Network/Other routes).
		The basic unit cost for LAs was derived as an average of actual unit costs for certain 'low-usage' LAs. This is supplemented where traffic and/or population per km exceed given thresholds. The respective contributions (2:1) were determined by professional judgement. There is also an allowance for the number of days with snow lying, based on a regression of actual winter maintenance expenditure.
All Other Services	District-Level Services	Because the services covered are so disparate, the only real choice for the client group was 'enhanced population'.
		The unit cost is based on a regression of actual expenditure/head against density and the *All Ages Social Index*. There is also an allowance for sparsity (5% of the total allocation), but the weights were derived by judgement.
		9.5% of the result for non-metropolitan district councils is re-allocated to the county council as a common amount per head, to take account of concurrent provision of some services.
	County-Level Services	Similar, but the *All Ages Social Index* is not used as an indicator. 2.5% of each county's SSA is reassigned to districts as a common amount per head.
	Rail (Met. areas)	Determined by the Secretary of State for Transport, and based on the length of route miles of local rail networks and infrastructure costs. Distributed between districts as a common amount per head.
	Flood Defence	Based on actual expenditure in the previous year, because LA expenditure is largely non-discretionary.
	Coast Protection	As for Flood Defence
	Revenue Interest Receipts	The control total is distributed pro-rata to the Total SSA, excluding Capital Financing.
	Boundary Changes	Where appropriate, pro-rata to the SSA of the authority from which the population was transfered.

Main Block	Sub-block	Method Used
Capital Financing	Debt Charges	Calculated by applying fixed interest and principal repayment rates to a notional figure for mid-year outstanding debt, excluding Housing, and then scaled to the control total.
	Interest on Capital Receipts	Distributed pro-rata to the Debt Charges SSA.
	Capital Expenditure Financed by Revenue (CERA)	Distributed pro-rata to the Credit Approvals indicator calculated for debt charges. This sub-block is discontinued from 1993-94.

Appendix 3

ASKING THE CUSTOMERS:
LOCAL AUTHORITY VIEWS OF THE SSA SYSTEM

BACKGROUND

1. As part of the programme of research, the Commission wished to understand the relationship between SSAs and LA budgeting and financial planning. This consisted of a theoretical and statistical analysis undertaken by the University of York and a survey of LAs in England and Wales. The study's advisory group suggested sending out the survey before the other work was completed, so that follow-up work could be carried out where a LA's response appeared to be of particular interest. A questionnaire was devised and agreed with the advisory group and with other relevant groups. Following consultation with the Welsh Office and Welsh LA Associations, it was agreed to send the same questionnaire to Welsh authorities, even though circumstances had been slightly different e.g. capping had not been imposed.

2. A copy of the questionnaire is attached as an Annex to this appendix. It was sent out at the beginning of November 1992, for return at the end of the month, and a reminder letter sent in early December to those LAs from whom no reply had been received.

RESPONSE

3. An overall response rate of nearly 80% was obtained, with 69% the lowest rate from any class of authority (Table A3.1).

Table A3.1
SURVEY RESPONSE

Description	Total no	Returns	%
London Boroughs	32	23	72%
Metropolitan Districts	36	25	69%
Counties	39	36	92%
English Shire Districts	296	228	77%
Joint Authorities	13	10	77%
Welsh Counties	8	6	75%
Welsh Shire Districts	37	30	78%
Total	462	358	78%

RESULTS

4. Two types of result were obtained: (a) answers to specific questions, and (b) other views and comments.

SPECIFIC QUESTIONS

5. The specific questions were:

Q2. **Setting the Overall Budget**
  (a) Factors influencing the budget process
  (b) Impact of capping

Q3. **Changes in Spending Needs**
  (a) Comparison with change in SSAs
  (b) Responses to under-funding

Q4. **Importance of Service-level SSAs**

Q5. **Uncertainty**
  (a) Planning horizon now vs. 5 years ago
  (b) Factors inhibiting long-term planning

Q7. **Acceptability of SSAs**
  (a) For grant distribution
  (b) As a basis for capping

6. The key finding was the impact that capping has had on LA budgeting behaviour. Capping limits are now far more important than other factors such as the LA's estimate of its spending needs and the resulting level of local taxation (Table A3.2). The current situation is very different from 2 years earlier, when spending needs were more important for most classes of authority. Most LAs said that they would have set higher budgets in 1992/93 in the absence of capping (Table A3.3). Only a few LAs spending well below SSA admitted that capping had increased their budgets, which appears to be at variance with the results of the statistical analysis presented in the main report.

7. Capping (and the level of SSA/RSG) were also cited by most LAs as the major contributors to uncertainty, hence inhibiting long term planning (Table A3.4). Thus, despite changes in the grant system which have improved stability and predictability, the number of LAs planning more than one year ahead has not increased over the last five years (Table A3.5).

8. The survey asked LAs whether service-level SSAs were important in setting service budgets. Most LAs do not attach great significance to them, although a number thought that the practice was likely to increase as budgets become increasingly tight (Table A3.6).

9. LAs were also asked to give their views about the acceptability of the current system of SSAs for distribution of RSG and as a basis for capping. While more than 40% of all LAs regard the system as acceptable for grant distribution, only very few authorities are satisfied with their role in capping (Table A3.7).

14

Table A3.2
MOST IMPORTANT FACTOR INFLUENCING BUDGET SETTING

		ENGLAND					WALES		ALL
		London Boroughs	Met. Districts	Counties	Shire Districts	Other LAs	Counties	Shire Districts	LAs
1990/91	LA estimate of spending need	39%	20%	64%	57%	40%	67%	67%	54%
	The LAs SSA	4%	8%	3%	8%	10%	17%	7%	7%
	Capping limits	30%	60%	19%	8%	40%	0%	3%	15%
	Impact on the community charge	22%	24%	19%	29%	0%	17%	37%	27%
1991/92	LA estimate of spending need	9%	4%	25%	43%	10%	33%	60%	37%
	The LAs SSA	13%	8%	11%	10%	0%	17%	13%	10%
	Capping limits	65%	84%	58%	12%	80%	50%	3%	27%
	Impact on the community charge	26%	12%	14%	37%	0%	0%	37%	31%
1992/93	LA estimate of spending need	9%	0%	22%	22%	0%	67%	43%	21%
	The LAs SSA	13%	4%	6%	12%	10%	0%	17%	11%
	Capping limits	70%	92%	72%	59%	90%	33%	40%	62%
	Impact on the community charge	22%	4%	8%	17%	0%	0%	17%	15%

Note: Columns may not add to 100% since more than one option could be selected as important

Table A3.3
BUDGET IN THE ABSENCE OF CAPPING

		London Boroughs	Met. Districts	Counties	Shire Districts	Other LAs	Counties	Shire Districts	ALL LAs
1990/91	Lower than actual budget	0%	4%	0%	0%	0%	17%	4%	1%
	About the same	36%	28%	63%	55%	40%	33%	54%	51%
	Higher than actual budget	45%	68%	23%	8%	50%	0%	7%	17%
	N/A	18%	0%	14%	38%	10%	50%	36%	31%
1991/92	Lower than actual budget	0%	4%	3%	0%	0%	0%	4%	1%
	About the same	36%	24%	31%	48%	10%	33%	43%	42%
	Higher than actual budget	55%	72%	56%	17%	90%	33%	18%	29%
	N/A	9%	0%	11%	35%	0%	33%	36%	27%
1992/93	Lower than actual budget	0%	0%	0%	2%	10%	0%	0%	1%
	About the same	23%	12%	28%	31%	10%	17%	25%	28%
	Higher than actual budget	64%	88%	64%	59%	80%	50%	57%	62%
	N/A	14%	0%	8%	8%	0%	33%	18%	9%

Table A3.4
FACTORS INHIBITING LONG TERM PLANNING

		ENGLAND					WALES		ALL
		London Boroughs	Met. Districts	Counties	Shire Districts	Other LAs	Counties	Shire Districts	LAs
No importance	Changes in spending requirements	4%	4%	17%	11%	10%	17%	0%	9%
	Levels of SSAs/RSG	0%	0%	6%	2%	0%	0%	0%	2%
	Capping limits	4%	0%	11%	8%	0%	0%	7%	7%
	Local Government Reorganisation	83%	80%	58%	26%	40%	0%	10%	36%
Limited importance	Changes in spending requirements	48%	60%	50%	47%	70%	67%	53%	50%
	Levels of SSAs/RSG	4%	8%	14%	15%	20%	0%	3%	13%
	Capping limits	9%	8%	11%	15%	0%	0%	17%	13%
	Local Government Reorganisation	17%	16%	31%	50%	30%	83%	43%	43%
Very important	Changes in spending requirements	48%	36%	33%	43%	20%	17%	47%	41%
	Levels of SSAs/RSG	96%	92%	81%	83%	80%	100%	97%	86%
	Capping limits	87%	92%	78%	76%	100%	100%	77%	80%
	Local Government Reorganisation	0%	4%	11%	24%	30%	17%	47%	21%

Table A3.5
PLANNING HORIZONS

		London Boroughs	Met. Districts	Counties	Shire Districts	Other LAs	Counties	Shire Districts	ALL LAs
Now	1 year	68%	56%	67%	52%	70%	83%	62%	57%
	2 years	9%	24%	14%	20%	10%	0%	28%	19%
	Longer	23%	20%	19%	28%	20%	17%	10%	24%
5 years ago	1 year	64%	48%	61%	57%	44%	83%	63%	58%
	2 years	18%	28%	11%	15%	33%	0%	17%	16%
	Longer	18%	24%	28%	28%	22%	17%	20%	26%

Table A3.6
IMPORTANCE OF SERVICE-LEVEL SSAs

	London Boroughs	Met. Districts	Counties	Shire Districts	Other LAs	Counties	Shire Districts	ALL LAs
No importance	61%	76%	71%	N/A	N/A	N/A	N/A	70%
Limited importance	35%	20%	26%	N/A	N/A	N/A	N/A	27%
Very important	4%	4%	3%	N/A	N/A	N/A	N/A	4%

Table A3.7
OVERALL ACCEPTABILITY

	London Boroughs	Met. Districts	Counties	Shire Districts	Other LAs	Counties	Shire Districts	ALL LAs
For distributing RSG	35%	28%	69%	41%	20%	100%	47%	43%
As a basis for capping	4%	4%	3%	7%	0%	17%	20%	8%

OTHER VIEWS AND COMMENTS

10. The other views and comments were very wide ranging and for the purpose of analysis were grouped into 4 main categories:

(a) Local Issues which were felt to disadvantage certain LAs

— Economic

— Environmental

— Demographic

— Geographical

— Financial

— Costs arising from local facilities or amenities

— Local initiatives

(b) The impact of SSAs on Budgeting and Financial Planning

— Constraints on LA actions

— Accountability

— Impact on planning

— Interpretation of SSAs

(c) Problems with the SSA Methodology

— Allocation methods

— Indicators

— Specific assessments

— Consultation process

— Control Totals

— What SSAs should take into account

— General issues

(d) Capping

— Acceptability

— Capping mechanisms

— Differential approaches

— Who should do it ?

— Need for more fundamental change

11. A summary of these views is given in the main report. A full analysis of all the results is contained in a separate document, published as Background Paper 8.8.

A3. Annex

THE COMMISSION'S SURVEY
SSAs AND LOCAL AUTHORITY FINANCIAL PLANNING

AUDIT COMMISSION SURVEY: SSAs AND LOCAL AUTHORITY FINANCIAL PLANNING

1. LOCAL AUTHORITY NAME:

2. SETTING THE OVERALL BUDGET

(a) What factors are most important in determining how the authority sets its overall budget?

Rank in order for each year: 1,2,3... (1=most important)	1990/91	1991/92	1992/93
What the LA estimates is necessary to spend to provide an appropriate standard of service			
What government estimates is necessary to provide a common standard of service i.e. the LA's SSA			
Limits on expenditure (capping criteria)			
The impact of spending on the community charge			
Other factors			
(please specify)			

(b) If there had been no expenditure limitation (capping), would your budget have been...

Please tick one item in each column		1990/91	1991/92	1992/93
Lower	1			
About the same	2			
Higher	3			
Not applicable	4			

3. CHANGES IN SSAs AND SPENDING REQUIREMENTS

(a) In comparison with changes in spending requirements, were the annual changes in SSAs...

Please tick one item in each column		1990/91	1991/92	1992/93
More than sufficient	1			
About right	2			
Insufficient	3			

(b) If changes in spending requirements have exceeded the changes in SSAs:

(i) are there any particular local circumstances which have contributed ?

and (ii) what has been your council's response:

Please tick each item that applies	
Cut spending plans	1
Use revenue reserves	2
Increase the community charge	3

Other actions (please specify)

4. SETTING BUDGETS FOR INDIVIDUAL SERVICES
(not to be completed by Shire Districts, Welsh Counties or single service authorities)

(a) To what extent are individual service SSAs used as a basis for setting service budgets ?

Please tick one item only	
Not at all	1
To a limited extent	2
Important consideration	3

(b) Are there any services where the SSA seems to be particularly low in comparison with spending needs ?

Please tick at most 5 items

Education			Personal Social Services					
	Under 5	1		Children	7	Fire & Civil Defence	12	
	Primary	2		Elderly (Dom)	8	Police	13	
	Secondary	3		Elderly (Resid)	9	Highway Maintenance	14	
	Post 16	4		Other	10	Other Services (District)	15	
	Other	5		In total	11	Other Services (County)	16	
	In total	6				Capital Financing	17	

If so, please give details of any particular local circumstances which you think may explain this.

5. THE IMPACT OF UNCERTAINTY

(a) What is the planning horizon for your council's revenue expenditure and how does this compare with 5 years ago ?

Please tick one item in each column		Now	5 years ago
1 year	1		
2 years	2		
Longer	3		

(b) How important is uncertainty about the following factors in inhibiting longer term planning by your council ?

Please score each item (0,1 or 2)	0 = no importance 1 = limited importance 2 = very important
Changes in spending requirements	
The level of SSAs/RSG allocations	
Capping criteria	
Local government re-organisation	
Other reasons	
(please specify)	

6. OTHER ISSUES

If you have any other comments on the impact of SSAs on the authority's financial arrangements, please make them here:

7. ALTERNATIVE APPROACHES

(a) In your view, are SSAs acceptable now as a basis for ...

Please tick one item in each row	Yes	No
Distributing Revenue Support Grant		
Capping		

| | | 1 | 2 |

(b) If you think SSAs are inappropriate for distributing Revenue Support Grant, what are the main reasons ?

(c) Recognising that the government insists on limiting council expenditure and needs a basis for doing so, do you have any particular views on how such a system should work?

Appendix 4

INSIDE THE BLACK BOX
TECHNICAL ISSUES CONCERNING THE SSA METHODOLOGY AND MODELS

1. This appendix attempts an evaluation of the current system of SSAs by considering the methodology and models used. It assesses the nature of errors which may arise within the system, and suggests how such errors might be minimised.

PROBLEMS WITH THE METHODOLOGY
MEASURING NEED TO SPEND

2. The DoE's definition of SSAs refers to a standard level of service. This is not defined. As a result it is difficult to find appropriate criteria by which to judge how well SSAs are performing their task. The definition suggests that the system should in some sense be *fair*, but this still leaves considerable room for interpretation. For example, in Education, it could mean equalising inputs (teachers per pupil, perhaps adjusted for need) or outcomes (e.g. attainment or improvement), each of which could lead to different distributions of resources. And it leaves open the question of *how* fair the system has to be i.e. how far inherent approximations and imperfections can be tolerated (which will depend on what the SSAs are being used for).

3. Nevertheless, it is possible to establish whether the allocation system has weaknesses which make it likely to systematically advantage or disadvantage particular local authorities (LAs), and, if so, where the potential areas of weakness are.

POTENTIAL FOR BIAS IN THE REGRESSION ESTIMATES

4. Many of the assessments are based on regression analysis. This statistical technique is powerful, but must be used in an appropriate way if the results are to be reliable. There are a number of potential problem areas. A key assumption made by government is that variation about the predicted regression line (residuals) is due to policy or efficiency differences between LAs, which can be ignored since it is only variations in need that matter. Problems can occur if these residuals are correlated with any of the indicator variables used in the model. If LAs which are relatively inefficient, or which choose to be high spenders for policy reasons, tend to be in areas where indicator scores are high, then the assessments may be distorted (Exhibit A4.1 – overleaf).

5. There are reasons to believe that such correlations might exist. Political control is certainly correlated with indices of social deprivation, such as the All Ages Social Index (Exhibit A4.2 – overleaf). It would therefore not be surprising if such correlation also affected policy variables, such as the level of services provided. Similarly, significant bias could be introduced into the coefficient estimates if London authorities, which tend to account for the more extreme indicator values, were more or less efficient than other authorities.

Exhibit A4.1
DANGERS OF USING ACTUAL COST DATA IN REGRESSIONS
If LAs which are relatively inefficient, or spend a lot relative to need, tend to be in areas where indicator scores are higher than average… then the results can be distorted.

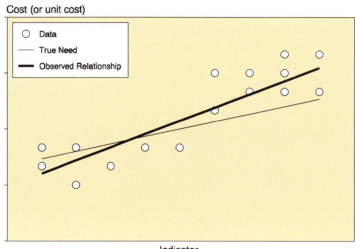

Source: Audit Commission

Exhibit A4.2
LINK BETWEEN INDICATORS AND POLITICAL CONTROL
Political control and social deprivation are closely correlated.

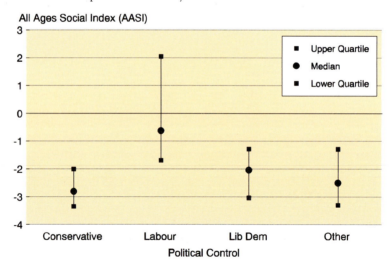

Source: DoE

6. Another potential problem is suggested by micro-economic theory, which predicts that in high cost areas, LAs will tend to provide a service at a lower standard or not at all. This may well be the reason why regression analysis was unable to detect a sparsity effect in the Other Services block regressions (it had to be added judgementally). The Commission's field-work also provided some evidence that such phenomena do occur in practice. For example, standards of service in refuse collection were lower in very rural areas, where unit costs were considerably higher, than in urban areas.

FEEDBACK

7. Another problem is that LA policy decisions, and in particular their budgeting behaviour, are increasingly constrained by government's expenditure limitation policies. Regressions based on historical expenditure, activity levels or unit costs will also reflect these pressures. Thus any imperfections in the GREs used to determine historical levels of grant might have been carried into the current SSA assessments; this danger could become more pronounced in future, when assessments come to be updated, because of the convergence of budgets and SSAs, which is identified in the main report.

8. This problem of 'feedback' is compounded by the high level of aggregation which occurs in the Other District Services assessment, because it accounts for the great majority of a LA's spending, and hence constraints on overall spending impact directly on the level of spending on this group of services. There are therefore serious doubts about whether these assessments will be able to be updated satisfactorily in future. Doing a regression on shire districts' expenditure, where this expenditure is constrained by having to spend at SSA, will no doubt result in similar coefficients – but it is hardly a confirmation that the formula is correct.

REGRESSION ASSUMPTIONS

9. Regression analysis also relies on the validity of a number of technical assumptions, such as the variation about the regression line being uniform. A number of the regressions tested failed this test and would create more reliable coefficients if transformed e.g. converting both dependent and independent variables of the Children's PSS Unit Cost regression to logarithms. Other analyses could also benefit[1].

10. Another desirable feature of regressions is that the indicators used should not be too highly correlated with each other (collinearity), because this can cause the resulting coefficients to be unreliable. There are examples where collinearity might be problematic. For example, density and All Ages Social Index, both indicators used in the Other District Services assessment, have a correlation coefficient of 0.89. The problem has been addressed in a number of cases by creating composite indicators, but this practice has not been adopted universally.

11. In the Children's PSS assessment, a composite indicator is used for the unit cost regression, but not for the Children at Risk analysis, which uses three individual variables which exhibit high inter-correlations (children in lone parent families, children of Income Support recipients and children living in rented accommodation). A further variable, relating to over-crowding, which had been identified as important in research commissioned by the DoE, was dropped because it 'added little to the explanatory power of the equation and its regression coefficient was negative'[2]. But where collinearity exists, lack of significance of a particular variable may not provide compelling evidence that it should be excluded from a model. It is often better to use standard corrective techniques than to exclude apparently insignificant variables from the regression[3]. Such methods could have been employed to enable the variable to be used in the equation and thus to make better use of the commissioned research.

---

1   B. Jatana, *Standard Spending Assessments – Regression Formulae Analysis*, Univ. of Surrey (Background Paper 8.9)

2   *Standard Spending Assessments: Background and Underlying Methodology*, DoE, 1990

3   For example, as described in David A. Belsey, *Conditioning Diagnostics – Collinearity and Weak Data in Regression*, 1991, Chapter 10

PROBLEMS WITH THE MODELS

12. In assessing the models, four areas have been identified where they may not be satisfactory. The indicators may be inadequate, the assessments may be too highly aggregated, the diversity of LAs may be too great or the wrong model type may have been selected.

INDICATORS MAY BE INADEQUATE

13. Thirty seven percent of authorities responding to the Commission's survey complained that SSAs were too insensitive to local need and circumstances. Many felt that indicators of social deprivation were inappropriate or too heavily weighted. For shire districts, this is often a reference to the use of the All Ages Social Index (AASI) in the Other District Services SSA. Many LAs find it difficult to conceive why social deprivation should be a significant indicator for the type of services provided at district level.

14. The analysis below demonstrates that AASI accounts for 28% of the amount distributed, after recasting the calculations so that the impact of all indicators is positive (Table A4.1). However, because the other indicators used in the assessment (density, sparsity) are highly correlated with AASI, more than 95% of the variation in the SSA can be explained by AASI alone (Exhibit A4.3).

Table A4.1
RELATIVE EFFECT OF INDICATORS IN THE OTHER DISTRICT SERVICES SSA

Indicator	Lowest Effect (any LA) £/adult	Highest Effect (any LA) £/adult	Weighted Average (all LAs) £/adult	Weighted Average (all LAs) %
Constant	52.86	52.86	52.86	47.1%
Density	0.00	73.68	18.33	16.3%
AASI	0.00	151.21	31.00	27.6%
Sparsity	0.00	37.15	5.53	4.9%
Area Cost Adjustment	0.00	53.66	4.58	4.1%
Total			112.30	100.0%

Source: Standard Spending Indicators (1992/93)

N.B.   Without adjustment, the AASI has a negative impact for some LAs

15. The Other Services SSA provides the strongest, but not the only, evidence that the range of indicators may be too narrow to characterise spending variations. When GREs were simplified, a number of indicators were lost (e.g. youth and total unemployment, heads of households in semi-skilled or unskilled occupations, households with 4 or more dependent children, elderly people with mobility problems or low income adjustment). It can be argued that such indicators added very little value to the formulae but simply increased their complexity. However, many LAs complain that there is now no proper allowance for economic rather than social deprivation. There is a powerful case for some measure of unemployment, which may be thought likely to influence spending on social services and leisure, as well as affecting levels of income achievable from fees and charges. There is no direct measure of health in the system, but

Exhibit A4.3
OTHER DISTRICT SERVICES SSA
More than 95% of the variation in the SSA can be explained by the single AASI indicator.

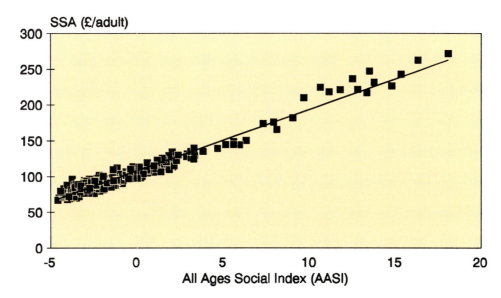

Source: Audit Commission

there is some evidence to show that Standardised Mortality Ratios (SMRs), potentially a stable and reliable indicator, can improve the fit of regression analyses[1].

16. On the other hand, the indicator *Persons without a bath or indoor WC* could be thought somewhat anachronistic, and its inclusion questioned. Measuring the proportion of people in shared accommodation is of benefit to areas with a high proportion of students in the population, but makes no contribution to identifying deprivation in areas where social problems are concentrated in particular estates of social housing. The 1991 Census will provide a potential source of new indicators, and should be examined to see whether improvements can be identified to address some of these issues.

17. Excluding the area cost adjustment, only 15 indicators (or 18 including individual components of composite indicators) are used to characterise variations in spending in the Education, PSS and All Other Services blocks, which account for nearly 80% of total SSAs (Exhibit A4.4 ~ overleaf). Some indicators occur in many different assessments: *Children in lone parent families* occurs in seven, and the related *Persons in lone parent families* in a further two.

18. The variety of the indicators used is even lower than it appears. Many directly or indirectly measure social deprivation and hence high levels of correlation exist between some of them. The three composite indicators are composed of a similar range of indicators and exhibit such high correlations that in practice their effect will be scarcely differentiable (Table A4.2). The effect of these inter-correlations is illustrated by the fact that the single AASI indicator can account for nearly 90% of the total variation in Education, PSS and Other Services SSAs, even though it is used directly in only 2 of the 12 assessments (Exhibit A4.5, overleaf).

---

1   *Dept. of Geography, Univ. of Salford, Standard Spending Assessments: A Report for Wigan MBC*

Exhibit A4.4
RANGE OF INDICATOR VARIABLES USED IN SSAs
Only 18 indicators, many of which are correlated, are used to characterise spending in services which account for nearly 80% of total SSAs.

Indicator	Education					Personal Social Services					All Other Services	
						Children		Elderly		Other		
	Primary	Secondary	Post 16	Under 5	Other	Risk	Cost	Residential	Domiciliary	Cost	District	County
Population Sparsity	✔	✔	✔								✔	✔
Ward-Weighted Density							■			✔	✔	✔
Annual Population Decline							■					
Children of Lone Parents	●	●	●	●	●	✔	■					
Children of Claimants	●	●	●	●	●	✔						
Children or HoH from NC/Pakistan[1]	●	●	●	●	●		■					
Children on Free School Meals	✔	✔										
Children in Rented Accommodation						✔						
Persons in Lone Parent Families										♦	♦	
Persons in Non-s/c Accommodation[2]							■			♦	♦	
Persons Without Private Bath/WC										♦	♦	
Persons in Crowded Accommodation										♦	♦	
Persons where HoH from NC/Pakistan[1]										♦	♦	
Elderly Living Alone								✔	✔			
Elderly Claimants								✔	✔			
Elderly in Independent Homes								✔				
Elderly Privately Renting									✔			
Elderly over 85									✔			

Notes: ✔ *indicator is directly used*

          ● *indicator is part of Additional Educational Needs composite indicator*

          ■ *indicator is part of Childrens Social Index composite indicator*

          ♦ *indicator is part of All Ages Social Index composite indicator*

          1 *Head of household born in the New Commonwealth or Pakistan*

          2 *Accommodation that is not self-contained*

Source: *Dept. of Geography, Univ. of Salford, Standard Spending Assessments: A Report for Wigan MBC*

Table A4.2
CORRELATIONS BETWEEN COMPOSITE INDICATORS

	AEN	CSI	AASI
Additional Educational Need (AEN)	~	0.89	0.93
Children's Social Index (CSI)	~	~	0.95

Source: Dept. of Geography, Univ. of Salford, Standard Spending Assessments: A Report for Wigan MBC

Exhibit A4.5
EDUCATION, PSS AND OTHER SERVICES SSA
Because the AASI indicator is correlated with many of the others, it can alone explain nearly 90% of the variation in the combined SSA for Education, PSS and Other Services.

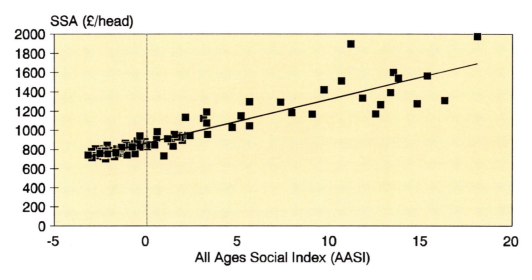

Note: County data adjusted for service responsibilities
Source: Standard Spending Indicators (1992/93)

19. Another potential problem with too narrow a range of indicators is that regressions might lead to relationships which consistently reward or disadvantage a similar set of LAs. If this were the case, regression residuals would be correlated, and would not display the 'swings and roundabouts' effect which would be expected if the residuals reflected simply the impact of random choice and efficiency factors. Examination of residuals from 6 regressions is consistent with this hypothesis (Exhibit A4.6(a) ~ overleaf). And analysis by LA class shows that Inner London boroughs, and, to a lesser extent, Metropolitan Districts have SSAs typically lower than historic spending levels, with the reverse true for Shire Counties (Exhibit A4.6(b) ~ overleaf). There are two possibilities: either that some LAs are indeed being systematically disadvantaged, and others advantaged, by the regressions, or that there are systematic policy or efficiency differences between classes of authority which lead to different levels of spending in relation to need in different classes of authority. It might be argued, for example, that residuals for Inner London boroughs and some Met. Districts tend to be negative because they are high spenders in relation to need. However, if this is the case, then the assumptions underlying the regression analyses (para 4) are invalid. In either case, there is a significant cause for concern about the validity of the assessments.

Exhibit A4.6
ANALYSIS OF REGRESSION RESIDUALS
(a) COMPARISON WITH EXPECTED DISTRIBUTION
The distribution of the residuals contains more outliers than expected...

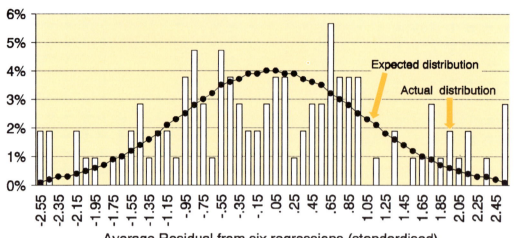

(b) ANALYSIS BY AUTHORITY CLASS
...and analysis by class reveals different patterns between classes.

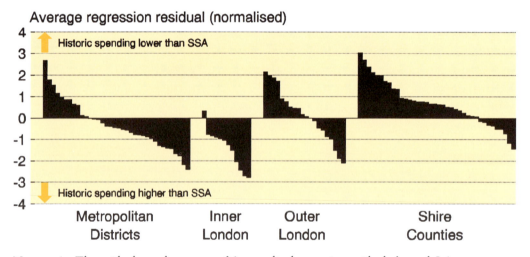

Notes: 1. *The residuals are the average of 6 normalised regression residuals for each LA*
2. *The regressions are Education: (a) Primary/Secondary unit costs, (b) Other Services unit costs, Personal Social Services: (c) Children's unit cost, (d) Elderly Residential client group, (e) Other Services unit costs, Other Services: (f) County-level services*

Source: *Dept. of Geography, Univ. of Salford, Standard Spending Assessments: A Report for Wigan MBC*

20. There are also some concerns with how the composite indicators have been created. The DoE sought guidance on the construction of indicators of social deprivation from Professor Bartholomew (LSE). He gave three main guidelines[1]. The constituent indicators should all:

---

1   *Prof. D J Bartholomew, Measuring Social Disadvantage and Additional Educational Needs, LSE*

(a) have 'nice' distributions (i.e. should be approximately normal)

(b) manifestly relate to social deprivation

(c) be directly relevant to the population under consideration

21. But these guidelines are not always obeyed. For example, the CSI indicator contains the variable *annual population decline* which is zero for most LAs, not directly relevant to children and can also be a sign of urban re-development rather than deprivation; it thus infringes all three criteria. And the 'ethnicity' indicators, which occur in all three composites, have very skewed distributions. The weightings of constituent indicators are also of some concern. For example, the weight on ethnicity in AEN was based on the relative values of coefficients in various regression analyses, which is a questionable practice if the variables are inter-correlated.

22. Another common complaint identified by the Commission's survey was that assessments are influenced too much by spending patterns based on past needs and may therefore take insufficient account of changes in needs. There may be some substance to these claims. Ten of the 18 indicators used in the Education, PSS and Other Services blocks (Exhibit A4.4) derive from the census, and hence can be as much as 13 years out of date. The DoE has favoured census variables because of their reliability, availability and freedom from potential manipulation by LAs, but timeliness is a significant counter-argument. It is no easy task to identify indicators which are relevant, up to date, based on objective data, free from potential manipulation and significant in terms of impact.

SERVICE ASSESSMENTS MAY BE TOO HIGHLY AGGREGATED

23. Models may suffer from being too highly aggregated i.e. the underlying structure which might be observable within the constituent elements is hidden when they are looked at together. The two main Other Services assessments (district-level and county-level) comprise about 30 individual services which were assessed individually within GREs. It is likely that some sensitivity is lost in the process of aggregation; in itself this does not demonstrate that aggregation is inappropriate. The question is whether the loss in sensitivity is compensated by improvements in simplicity and administrative convenience. The answer will not be easy to agree on -- losses in sensitivity can disadvantage (and advantage) some LAs, while administrative convenience benefits those who are operating the system. In terms of simplicity, disaggregation may increase the level of detail but assist understanding by relating indicators more closely to factors which appear relevant.

24. The Scottish and Welsh systems both use more disaggregated assessments of district-level services similar to GREs, with 24 and 27 separate assessments respectively. The Commission's analysis of allocations data from the Scottish system provides a measure of the potential impact of disaggregation (Annex to Appendix 5). For Scotland, a noticeable loss in sensitivity, expressed in potentially significant changes in distribution of grant, occurs if the number of assessments is reduced from 24 to below 9. The loss happens because a number of services of significant size have different allocation patterns; attempting to force them into a common pattern therefore alters the distribution. The Scottish results do not justify a categorical statement about the ideal level of disaggregation for the English system. But they do suggest that the current highly aggregated

assessments may be less sensitive than they could be; even separating out 5 or so assessments could make a significant improvement in sensitivity.

25. At the level of county services the case for disaggregation is less clear. Although the Welsh and Scottish systems are more disaggregated than the English, it does not appear that increasing disaggregation in England for County services would significantly alter the distribution, but it would increase complexity.

THE RANGE OF LAs MAY BE TOO WIDE

26. Examination of residuals from *individual* regressions should reveal a similar random pattern for each type of authority. However, a number of assessments reveal distinct geographical patterns. In the Other County Services assessments, virtually all counties 'gain' (in the sense of having a higher estimate than actual expenditure) and virtually all metropolitan districts 'lose' (Exhibit A4.7). This is a clear indication that the model is mis-specified. There are similar problems within the Personal Social Services (PSS) assessments. In the Children's Unit Cost regression, London LAs tend to lose, while metropolitan districts gain, and the Other Social Services regression favours shire counties.

Exhibit A4.7
REGRESSION RESIDUALS: OTHER COUNTY-LEVEL SERVICES
The regression appears to favour Shire Counties and disadvantage Met.Districts.

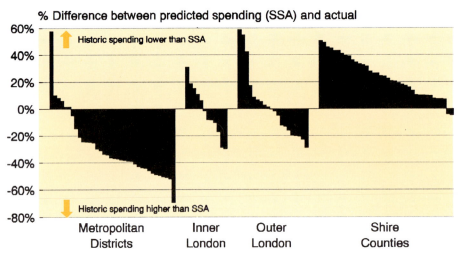

Source: Dept. of Geography, Univ. of Salford, Standard Spending Assessments: A Report for Wigan
       MBC

27. A 'dummy' variable, indicating the authority class, can be introduced into the model, which in effect allows each authority class to have its own constant term in the regression. Such changes tend to improve some of the fits, which is helpful provided that there are good grounds for believing that the model should be of this type. But inappropriate use of this technique can hide a mis-specified model.

28. Another test of model suitability is to perform separate regressions for different classes of authority. The resulting coefficients should be similar in each case. But in the Other District Services assessment, where the residuals have no obvious geographical pattern, very different results emerge (Box A4.A). This suggests that the apparent fit of the formula over all districts

The relationship which is the basis of the Other District Services (ODS) assessment was derived by a weighted regression of outturn 1987/88 expenditure/head, adjusted for London costs, against ward-weighted density and the All Ages Social Index (AASI) (the sparsity factor was added later, with judgementally selected weights). To test the robustness of the relationship, separate regressions were carried out for Shire Districts, Met. Districts and London Boroughs, and London was further split into Inner/Outer Boroughs.

The following table shows the resulting regression coefficients and the goodness of fit statistic (% of variance explained).

REGRESSION COEFFICIENTS AND GOODNESS OF FIT

	Constant	AASI	Density	Fit
All LAs	51.7	4.17	4.55	64%
Shire Districts	52.4	3.13	3.06	43%
Met. Districts	69.3	1.96	-0.47	11%
London Boroughs	37.4	4.68	6.63	57%
Outer London	49.8	4.19	2.99	77%
Inner London	176.4	8.36	-11.74	12%

The difference between the results for the 3 main authority types is substantial. Not only are the coefficients different, but the goodness of fit is worse in all cases. The regression for Met. Districts is not statistically significant.

The London Boroughs regression is the best of the three, but even here the density coefficient is very different from the original. It is clear from the Inner/Outer London analysis that the overall picture for London disguises the underlying details. The Outer London relationship is similar to that for all LAs, and with an even better fit. The Inner London regression is completely different -- a very poor fit, with a negative density coefficient.

Overall, the ODS regression appears plausible because there is a large variation in spending patterns between different types of authority. The two indicators, density and the social index, are effective at distinguishing between different types of authority e.g. an Inner London borough vs a shire district, but are nothing like as good at predicting spending patterns in similar types of authority. The variance actually explained by the regression is therefore much less than the overall goodness of fit figure implies. In particular, the regression says nothing about spending patterns in Met. Districts or Inner London Boroughs. This suggests that using a single relationship to cover all LAs is inappropriate.

occurs because the two indicators (density and the All Ages Social Index) are effective at distinguishing between *very different* types of authority e.g. an Inner London borough compared with a typical shire district. However, they are not good at predicting spending patterns in *similar* types of authority and, in some cases, do not appear to explain spending patterns at all, in particular in Metropolitan Districts or Inner London boroughs. At best, the model should only be used for certain classes of authority.

29. Some work has been done using the techniques of analysis of covariance and cluster analysis to examine whether this phenomenon is a general feature of assessments[1]. It suggests that Inner London boroughs form a distinct group and that separate regression lines are normally appropriate. On the other hand, Outer London Boroughs, Met. Districts and Shire Counties (or Shire Districts, depending on the assessment) do tend to form a coherent group where a single analysis is acceptable. There are some indications that some Outer London boroughs have characteristics similar to those of Inner London boroughs for some assessments, but not in all cases. One problem with a separate Inner London group is that the number of LAs is rather small. Nevertheless, tackling this problem may be preferable to allowing coefficients to be distorted.

30. There is further support for this view from analysis of the level of influence of particular LAs on regressions. The influence individual data points exert on the regression can be measured by a statistic called leverage. If it is too high (typically twice the average), it suggests that some of the regression assumptions may not hold. Work done at Salford University[2] and elsewhere[1] shows that very high leverages do occur, principally among London LAs (Exhibit A4.8~overleaf).

MODELS MAY BE INAPPROPRIATE

31. One test of the adequacy of regression-based models is the statistical goodness of fit. Although, for reasons outlined earlier, a good fit does not guarantee an appropriate model, lack of fit suggests that the model may be inappropriate. Some of the goodness of fit statistics would normally be considered unsatisfactory ~ the worst example being the Potential Elderly Domiciliary Client Group regression, which explains only 12% of the variance. Although this model is untypical[3], the fit is very poor. In the Other Education regression, 16 LAs (15% of those modelled) have residuals in excess of 50% of the estimated value. In themselves, these are not conclusive evidence of a problem. The residual variation may be due to large policy or efficiency differences. The Commission's own work has shown that efficiency variations are often of the order of 1:3 between best and worst. Nevertheless, the poorer results do give some cause for concern.

32. Linear models (those which consist of weighted sums of indicators) are the norm for most assessments; this choice is essentially pragmatic. It is easy to find weightings for indicators in linear models through regression analysis. But there is no theoretical reason why models should be of this form. There is some evidence to suggest that non-linear models might be appropriate for some assessments[2]. But use of increasingly complex statistical devices to achieve a better fit

---

1   *B.Jatana, Standard Spending Assessments ~ Regression Formulae Analysis, Univ. of Surrey (Background Paper 8.9)*

2   *Dept. of Geography, Univ. of Salford, Standard Spending Assessments: A Report for Wigan MBC*

3   *The model used the 1985 General Household Survey to regress estimated domiciliary care costs for individuals against social and demographic indicators. For many of the individuals, the cost would have been zero.*

Exhibit A4.8

LEVERAGE OF LONDON AUTHORITIES IN REGRESSIONS
Very high leverages occur, principally among London LAs.

Definition:	Leverage measures the influence of each data point (LA) on the regression model
Problem:	High leverages (twice the average value) suggest that the LA does not satisfy the assumptions of the model
Results:	Many London LAs have leverages in excess of three times the average value (see Table), but few LAs outside London do

Primary/Secondary Education Unit Cost		Children's PSS Unit Cost		Elderly Residential PSS Client Group		Other Social Services Unit Cost		All Other Services: District Unit Cost		All Other Services: County Unit Cost	
Authority	L	Authority	L	Authority	L	Authority	L	Authority	L	Authority	L
Haringey	9.7	Lambeth	20.4	Kensington	16.9	Hackney	21.0	Hackney	19.6	Islington	20.7
ILEA	9.4	Hammersmith	20.0	Westminster	11.9	Hammersmith	17.0	Hammersmith	16.9	Westminster	18.5
Brent	6.8	Haringey	19.7	Camden	6.9	Lambeth	15.1	Islington	16.5	Hammersmith	18.3
Newham	6.7	Kensington	17.8	Tower Hamlets	5.7	Haringey	14.0	Haringey	16.3	Kensington	18.1
Manchester	5.4	Westminster	17.1	Sefton	5.2	Newham	12.1	Westminster	15.5	Hackney	16.6
Birmingham	5.1	Hackney	13.7	Hackney	3.2	Islington	11.6	Kensington	14.5	Southwark	13.1
Wolverhampton	3.5	Islington	11.5	Liverpool	3.1	Brent	11.4	Lambeth	14.4	Tower Hamlets	12.2
		Wandsworth	11.1			Wandsworth	10.4	Brent	12.4	Camden	11.4
		Camden	10.8			Kensington	10.0	Newham	11.8	Lambeth	10.5
		Brent	8.0			Camden	8.8	Southwark	10.9	Newham	10.1
		Newham	6.8			Tower Hamlets	7.9	Wandsworth	10.2	Wandsworth	8.2
		Southwark	6.3			Westminster	7.2	Tower Hamlets	10.2	Brent	4.9
		Lewisham	6.0			Southwark	6.0	Camden	10.0	Haringey	4.8
		Tower Hamlets	4.9			Ealing	5.2	Leicester	6.5	Lewisham	3.9
		Waltham Forest	3.2			Waltham Forest	4.0	Ealing	5.7	Waltham Forest	3.3
		Ealing	3.1			Lewisham	3.4	Blackburn	5.7		
								Kingswood	5.5		
								Sutton	5.0		
								Slough	4.5		
								Waltham Forest	4.4		
								Lewisham	4.1		
								Bexley	3.9		
								Blackpool	3.6		
								Hove	3.6		
								Wolverhampton	3.5		

L Leverage

Non-London Authority

Source: Dept. of Geography, Univ. of Salford, Standard Spending Assessments: A Report for Wigan MBC

to the data can result in opaque models which bear no obvious link with reality. It also places much reliance on the data being fitted, which may not be justified, as shown above.

33. In some circumstances, there are reasons for supposing that a more complex form of model might be appropriate. For example, the need to provide a specified standard of response to fire calls might be expected to lead to a complex relationship between Fire Service expenditure and the range of potential indicators, such as fire-risk gradings, alarm calls, and the local geography. While the standard (linear) relationship may be satisfactory for the majority of LAs, it might give rise to serious problems for 'outliers' – those LAs most different from the others.

CONCLUSIONS

34. Creating reliable and fair SSAs is a formidable task. There are many substantial problems, not least the key assumption underlying the regression analyses concerning the randomness of historic spending patterns in terms of choice and efficiency. The analysis presented here suggests that these problems might well lead to models with wrong coefficients, even where the model has been specified correctly. Does this matter? Clearly, it will mean that some LAs may be systematically disadvantaged compared to others. How acceptable this is depends both on the size of the errors and how the SSAs are used.

35. The main report shows that the most demanding use of SSAs is their rôle in capping. The DOE has argued that the system contains an allowance for imprecision because budget cuts are not required for spending within 12.5% of SSA. This takes no account of inflation, which could be viewed as reasonable if LA budgets were well in excess of SSA levels, as they were in 1990/91. However, for 1991/92 and 1992/93, aggregate LA spending has been within 1% of SSA[1], so it is arguable that some allowance for inflation could be justified. The capping limits for 1993/94 are such that for LAs to maintain real spending levels (assuming inflation of around 1.75%), they would have to set budgets within 5% of SSA (Exhibit 6, main report). This provides the context for the discussion about the size of likely errors in the existing system.

SIZE OF ERRORS

36. It is necessary to distinguish between the different types of error which can occur:

(a) prediction errors, due to random variation of the dependent variable about the modelled relationship

(b) systematic error (bias) or distortion in the model

(c) inadequacies in the model

(d) local circumstances which could not reasonably be expected to be allowed for in a model.

37. Type (a) errors are unavoidable, but type (b) & (c) errors can be minimised by adopting best statistical practice and by making every effort to ensure that models are appropriate and take account of all relevant factors. Type (d) errors can be addressed, but only outside the modelling

---

1   *Peter Smith, Local Government Expenditure and Standard Spending Assessments: A Statistical Analysis*
     (Background Paper 8.2).

process, for example by creating a process of negotiation which is better informed by local knowledge and allows a measure of discretion about how assessment formulae are applied.

38. Type (a) errors derive from the fact that statistical methods are of necessity imprecise, meaning that model coefficients can only be estimated within certain confidence limits, and, in the case of regression analysis, the size of the confidence limits depends on how good a statistical fit to the data is achieved by the model. When models are used in formulae for calculating SSAs, these have bigger effects for LAs whose indicator values are towards the extremes, because these will amplify any errors in the indicator weightings. The size of these 'prediction errors' can be calculated directly from the results of the related regression analysis. For example, in the case of the Other District Services regression (based on density and the All Ages Social Index), the standard deviation of the prediction errors varies from about 1.5% to 5.5%, depending on the type of authority (Table A4.3).

Table A4.3
STANDARD DEVIATION OF PREDICTION ERRORS: OTHER DISTRICT SERVICES

Authority Type	Minimum	Maximum
Shire Districts	1.4%	5.5%
Met. Districts	1.4%	3.0%
London Boroughs	1.6%	4.3%

Source: Audit Commission

39. There is also evidence that type (b) errors are also likely. Such errors could arise from model bias if the randomness assumption in relation to choice and efficiency is wrong. An idea of the size of the potential problem can be gained from reworking the regression analysis, using for illustrative purposes an assumption that all London LAs spend on average 10% more in relation to need than other authorities (and hence that per capita spending is reduced by 10% for London LAs prior to calculation). Such a change would result in SSAs for London and Met. Districts lower by an average of 4% and 1% respectively and those for Shire Districts higher by an average of 2%, but with considerable variation within each class (Table A4.4).

Table A4.4
THE IMPACT OF 10% 'OVER-SPENDING' BY LONDON LAs
PREDICTION BIAS: OTHER DISTRICT SERVICES

Class	Minimum	Average	Maximum
Shire Districts	-6.0%	-1.7%	4.3%
Met. Districts	-1.5%	1.1%	3.8%
London Boroughs	-0.2%	4.2%	7.0%

N.B. *Positive %s mean that unadjusted SSAs are higher than 'corrected' values*

Source: Audit Commission

40. The combined impact of both types of error can also be derived for each authority by calculating a confidence limit related to the prediction errors added to (or subtracted from) the prediction bias. This takes account of the fact that the highest values of bias do not necessarily coincide with the highest prediction errors. The results show that some SSAs might be over-stated

by as much as 13%, while others could be under-stated by the same amount (Table A4.5). Other assumptions on the size of any bias, and the authority class or classes involved, would of course give different results.

Table A4.5
COMBINED PREDICTION ERRORS AND BIAS: OTHER DISTRICT SERVICES

Class	95% Confidence Interval	
	Minimum	Maximum
Shire Districts	-13.2%	11.1%
Met. Districts	- 5.8%	8.5%
London Boroughs	- 7.3%	12.5%

N.B.   Positive %s mean that unadjusted SSAs are higher than 'corrected' values
Source: Audit Commission

41. While the assumption made above about bias cannot be proved realistic, it seems likely that some effect of this sort exists. And the figures take no account of type (c) errors i.e. they assume that the model is perfectly specified. In practice, this is unachievable, although it is impossible to give any precise idea of the effect of errors due to mis-specification, which will any case vary from assessment to assessment. However, the evidence presented does suggest that this could be a significant source of additional errors. Comparing these figures with capping limits, it is reasonable to conclude that it is likely that some LAs will be significantly advantaged or disadvantaged by SSAs for Other District Services. This is therefore also true for the SSA as a whole for shire district authorities.

42. A similar exercise can be done for regressions relating to other assessments, giving broadly similar results for the regressions tested, with Shire Counties displaying the same sort of results as Shire Districts did in the Other District Services regressions, under the same assumptions (Table A4.6).

43. It is not possible to be categorical about the implications for the total SSAs for multi-purpose authorities from such a small sample of assessments. However, if it is assumed that other assessments also followed the same pattern as Other District Services, and that the assessments were largely independent, then the 'swings and roundabouts' effect would mean that the confidence limits for total SSAs for multi-purpose authorities would on average have prediction errors (type (a)) of about a third the size of individual assessments[1] but with bias (type (b) errors) of a similar order. If bias were as assumed here, then the pattern of confidence limits for each authority type would be similar to that of individual assessments, but about half the size. If assessments did exhibit a degree of inter-correlation, as suggested above (paras 5, 14-19), then the figures would be a little higher.

44. When the results are applied to the use of SSAs for capping, there is some justification for giving shire districts (and single-purpose police or fire authorities) a larger allowance above SSA than multi-purpose authorities. Given the relative sizes of such authorities, any 'cost' to the

---

1   *The figure of a third is derived from the square root of the sums of squares of the 21 individual control totals for 1992/93, expressed as proportions of Total Standard Spending, reflecting the assumption that the variance of the SSA is the sum of the variances of the individual SSAs, and that these are proportional to the size of the SSA.*

Table A4.6
COMBINED PREDICTION ERRORS AND BIAS: VARIOUS ASSESSMENTS

| | | 95% Confidence Intervals | | | | | |
| | | Prediction Error | | Bias | | Combined | |
Assessment	Authority Type	Min	Max	Min	Max	Min	Max
Other PSS	Met. Districts	2.1%	3.7%	-3.6%	2.4%	-10.9%	7.0%
	London	2.1%	3.9%	-4.0%	6.0%	-11.8%	13.5%
	Shire Counties	2.4%	4.2%	-4.6%	-0.7%	-13.0%	4.1%
Children's PSS	Met. Districts	3.3%	5.9%	-4.0%	2.6%	-15.9%	9.8%
(Unit Cost)	London	3.3%	5.8%	-2.4%	6.0%	-11.8%	17.6%
	Shire Counties	4.0%	6.8%	-5.1%	-1.1%	-18.8%	8.6%
Other County–Level	Met. Districts	2.4%	5.1%	-5.8%	2.0%	-16.1%	7.0%
Services	London	2.4%	3.9%	-1.2%	6.3%	- 7.0%	14.1%
	Shire Counties	2.8%	6.6%	-8.5%	-0.9%	-21.8%	4.8%
Elderly Residential	Met. Districts	1.7%	10.5%	-6.5%	1.8%	-27.6%	14.5%
	London	2.1%	7.9%	-3.1%	3.7%	-14.2%	17.5%
	Shire Counties	1.9%	10.5%	-7.6%	1.0%	-28.6%	13.4%

Source: Audit Commission

larger authorities in tighter capping criteria would be relatively small. And, given that SSAs can as easily be over-stated as under-stated, there is scope to challenge the practice of allowing LAs to increase spending without limit provided that the resulting budget is less than SSA. Some limit on budget increases for such authorities would appear to be more consistent with the relative tightness of the regime for LAs above SSA.

MINIMISING ERRORS

45. The final section explores the potential for minimising the errors of the type described. A number of improvements have already been suggested in the text. Apart from these, there is scope for research designed to understand the factors which influence activity levels and unit costs in different LA circumstances. As part of this study, work of this kind was commissioned from KPMG Management Consulting to try to identify cost drivers for particular services in an attempt to distinguish choice and efficiency factors from costs reflecting underlying needs[1]. The main drivers were identified as the availability of resources, historic spending levels, the statutory framework governing service delivery and provision by other agencies. But for the most part, information was not readily available in a form which allowed any clear identification of reasons for cost differences between authorities.

---

1   KPMG *Management Consulting, Relationship between Local Authority Budgets, Activities and Standard Spending Assessments (SSAs). Summary (Background Paper 8.1).*

46. A more detailed study than could be undertaken in the time available to the Commission has been commissioned by the Department of Health and is being carried out by the Personal Social Services Research Unit at the University of Kent. Interim results suggest that, in some circumstances, cost and activity drivers can be successfully identified, and, in particular, that it might be possible to disentangle policy and efficiency differences from those due to local circumstances. This work provides a contrast to approaches used to derive unit costs in the current assessments, where the emphasis has typically been on identifying simple models to explain historic aggregate expenditure.

47. The drawback of an approach based on identifying cost and activity drivers is that, in comparison with purely statistical methods, much research may be required, particularly where service levels vary markedly and where service standards are not consistently defined across authorities. Such work is expensive. Even comparisons of a small number of authorities can take a long time because the analysis has to be very detailed, and is complicated by the fact that different LAs structure their organisations in different ways and that there are considerable differences in the information available. And because of changing LA practices, the results may be valid for a limited period of time. Nevertheless, where the assessments concerned are subject to considerable doubt, as many are, this sort of effort may well be justified if only on the basis of a sample of authorities.

48. There is another potential role for such work. Any viable system should have a means of assessing how well it is performing its task, so that corrections or fine-tuning can be made. But there is currently no means of validating SSAs. Complaints about unfairness are met with assurances about the appropriateness of the methods employed rather than the results. This allows the possibility that errors in the system can remain without identification or correction. Where the assessments are most controversial, or where they distribute a large amount of money, some check on the methodology seems desirable, particularly in helping to 'explain' large model residuals. The methods described in the previous paragraph should be considered for this purpose, even if they are not used to create the models in the first place.

Appendix 5

NOT THE ONLY WAY
A REVIEW OF OTHER UK FUNDING SYSTEMS

1. This appendix looks at a wide range of alternative methods of allocating centrally-provided funding to a number of lower-tier organisations in the UK. Systems covered include the equivalent of SSAs in Wales and Scotland, and other revenue funding systems within the UK: Hospital & Community Health Services (HCHS), Family Health Service Authorities (FHSAs), the Universities Funding Council (UFC), the Polytechnics & Colleges Funding Council (PCFC), the Higher Education Funding Council for England (HEFCE, which replaces UFC & PCFC in 1993/94), and Training and Enterprise Councils (TECs). The systems for allocating capital funding for housing to LAs and Housing Associations also have features of interest.

A TYPOLOGY OF SYSTEMS

2. The approach adopted is to produce a categorisation of the various systems and then to explore why it is that different systems should adopt different types of allocation rules. The lessons which emerge from these systems are used to throw light on some of the problems with SSAs identified in Appendix 4.

3. Most systems fall into one of two groups: those where the main aim is equalisation (to compensate for differences in needs and/or resources) and those where the principal objective is the control of expenditure (Exhibit A5.1 – overleaf). This classification is not mutually exclusive, since equalisation systems can have a control function. The first group are typically formula-based systems, which vary in terms of how the formulae have been derived. Some are principally empirical (i.e. derived by comparison with historic levels of funding), while others are more normative (i.e. based on an assessment of factors which should theoretically affect spending). Some are a mixture of the two. Another group is characterised by formulae which are subject to discretionary modification. The control systems are largely characterised by a 'core and margin' approach where the core, a high percentage of the previous year's funding, is supplemented by a margin typically allocated by means of a bidding process. There has been a recent trend, in equalisation and in control systems, to link part of the funding with performance. This applies particularly to TECs and to research funding in higher education; the Audit Commission has recently proposed the extension of this principle to the administration of Housing Benefit[1].

EQUALISATION SYSTEMS

4. Equalisation systems tend to begin with a division on the basis of relevant population, but the formulae are modified according to suitable measures of local needs.

---

1   *Remote Control, Audit Commission, 1993*

Exhibit A5.1

A TYPOLOGY OF UK FUNDING SYSTEMS

Most systems fall into one of two groups.

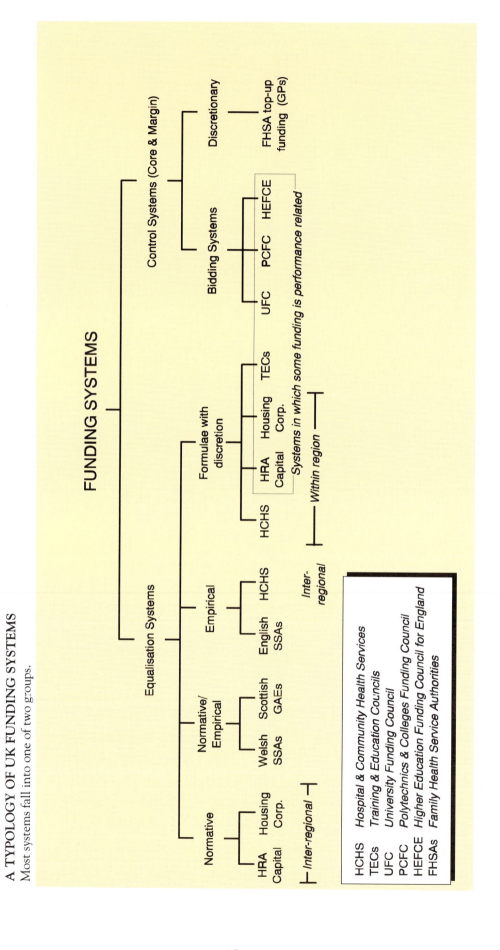

FUNDING SYSTEMS

Equalisation Systems

Normative

- HRA Capital
- Housing Corp.

⊢ *Inter-regional* ⊣

Normative/ Empirical

- Welsh SSAs
- Scottish GAEs

Empirical

- English SSAs
- HCHS

⊢ *Inter-regional* ⊣

Control Systems (Core & Margin)

Formulae with discretion

- HCHS
- HRA Capital
- Housing Corp.
- TECs

Systems in which some funding is performance related

⊢ *Within region* ⊣

Bidding Systems

- UFC
- PCFC
- HEFCE

Discretionary

- FHSA top-up funding (GPs)

HCHS *Hospital & Community Health Services*
TECs *Training & Education Councils*
UFC *University Funding Council*
PCFC *Polytechnics & Colleges Funding Council*
HEFCE *Higher Education Funding Council for England*
FHSAs *Family Health Service Authorities*

42

Normative Formulae

5. Housing capital funding is distributed initially to DoE regions on the basis of normative formulae. For LAs, the Generalised Needs Index (GNI), a weighted index of eleven measures of housing deprivation, is used to produce the initial regional allocation, and a similar formula, the Housing Needs Index (HNI), performs the same task for Housing Corporation funds. Government can modify the operation of the formulae by adjusting the weightings of the various elements of the indices.

Normative/Empirical Formulae

6. The Scottish Grant Aided Expenditure (GAE) system and Welsh SSA systems contain both normative and empirical elements[1]. These both feature assessments where the allocation is made on the basis of *primary needs indicators* alone, which have no link with past expenditure. Most primary needs indicators are based on population. But some use information which is relevant to a particular service. For example, costs of maintaining crematoria are allocated pro-rata to the number of cremations. But some assessments also use secondary indicators and the weightings for these are almost always found from regression analyses of historic expenditure. (The Welsh system also has a *tier split* calculation, to divide the total funding between counties and districts, which largely reflects the historic position.)

Empirically-Derived Formulae

7. The English SSA system is more dependent on historic patterns of spending. Most assessments are based on analyses which attempt to explain historic spending patterns in terms of a number of indicators, although calculations like those for Highways or Additional Educational Needs have a normative character. From 1977 to 1990, the Resource Allocation Working Party (RAWP) formula, based on *catchment* populations, distributed HCHS monies within the NHS. It was replaced in 1990/91 by the weighted capitation formula, based on *resident* populations (consistent with the NHS reforms), announced in the White Paper *Working for Patients*. In the RAWP formula, weighted population figures for each of the fourteen English regions acted as long-term targets for resource distribution. The weights were related to the region's age and sex distribution, condition-specific Standardised Mortality Ratios (SMRs) and regional pay cost variations. The new formula uses a simpler set of weightings for age, morbidity (measured by the all-causes SMR) and cost variations. These weights were derived empirically via ward-level NHS utilisation rates.

Formulae Subject to Discretion

8. Although the RAWP process and its successor brought regions quite close to their targets (11 of the 14 regions are within 1% in 1993/94), differences at district level are much wider. Progress towards targets at district level is therefore difficult, and regions have needed to use their discretion to manage the process satisfactorily. It will be a number of years before all districts are close to their target. There remain widespread doubts about whether weighted capitation captures the health consequences of socio-economic factors at district level. This year's review will use

---

1   *Details of how the Scottish and Welsh systems operate are given in the relevant Background Papers listed in Appendix 8.*

data from the 1991 Census to look again at the relationship between measures of morbidity and the use of health services.

9. Sixty percent of LA housing capital is distributed within regions by DoE Regional Controllers on a discretionary basis. In taking their decisions, they take into account existing commitments and also performance-related criteria in that they reward LAs which have well-prepared housing strategies in line with government policy. A similar mechanism works within the Housing Corporation, although the discretionary proportion is somewhat lower.

10. The formula to allocate money between the regional TECs is essentially normative, since total training weeks are related to the numbers of unemployed and school-leavers, but has a historic element, since unit costs reflect past expenditure and profit. A similar pattern operates within regions, but regions also apply their discretion in arriving at budgets for individual TECs. There is also a performance-related element since the payment system rewards the number of National Vocational Qualifications (NVQs) achieved.

CONTROL SYSTEMS

11. Some systems to control spending are not formula-based. These typically use a 'core and margin' approach. They apply to systems where funding needs to be stable over time and this is achieved by guaranteeing a high percentage in real terms of the previous year's funding (the core), and supplementing this with additional funds (the margin), usually intended to encourage good performance. For example, the Universities Funding Council (UFC) set a core of 98.5% for funding of teaching and a margin which rewarded the number of fees-only students. The Polytechnics and Colleges Funding Council (PCFC) set a core of 90%, and allowed organisations to bid on unit prices etc. for the remainder. Both these organisations will be replaced in 1993/94 by the Higher Education Funding Council for England (HEFCE), which proposes to base competition beyond a 98% core on average unit of council funding per enrolled student. But the use of performance as the main criterion for research funding means that there is a greater degree of discretion in the overall funding of Higher Education than a core of 98% would suggest.

12. FHSAs have discretion to distribute about 10% of their annual funding either to meet additional needs (e.g. in deprived areas) or to stimulate innovation in GP practices. Most is used to pay for additional staff – particularly practice managers and practice nurses, although IT equipment and improved premises can also be funded in this way. This acts as an additional margin above the nationally-agreed formula for GP payments defined as part of the 1990 GP contract.

LESSONS FROM OTHER SYSTEMS

13. This section draws out some general principles about funding systems from these examples in order to throw light on some of the problems for SSAs identified earlier. The lessons are:

Lesson 1:   Different purposes demand different methods

Lesson 2:   Size limits sensitivity

Lesson 3:   Disaggregation improves sensitivity

44

LESSON 1: DIFFERENT PURPOSES DEMAND DIFFERENT METHODS

14. The most striking feature of the typology is the range of different approaches employed. The differences are not accidental; the purpose of the system has a considerable influence on the choice of allocation system. The fundamental distinction is between systems to *equalise capability*, involving consideration of needs and resources, and those which seek to *control expenditure* within tight limits.

15. Equalisation systems seek to identify factors which explain variations in spending needs, and hence tend to be formulaic. Differences between actual spending and the formulae are often assumed to be principally due to differences in local policies or efficiency. However, it is inevitable that formulae will be imperfect and systems tend to contain some way of avoiding the consequent problems. A common expedient is the use of discretion. For example, the strict operation of the HCHS formula is modified both at an inter-Regional level and within regions to ensure that allocations do not diverge too much from historic levels of funding. TEC funding works in a similar way although the discretion also serves to reward performance, and much the same can be said about the allocation of housing capital.

16. Control systems are more concerned with the control of total expenditure and providing a stable financial environment for recipient organisations. UFC and PCFC allocations have been based largely on previous expenditure because of the benefits for planning and stability. And the national rather than local pattern of demand for Higher Education makes local assessment of need a lower priority. The purpose has been different, giving rise to a different method of allocation.

17. LA funding systems within the UK differ from other equalisation systems in that they are wholly formula-based. The flexibility to cope with imperfections in the formulae has traditionally been provided by specific grants or by the ability to raise revenue locally, but this latter method of increasing expenditure is now not available to some LAs as capping is increasingly tightly imposed. The pressures are higher in England because the settlement per head is lower; further, the Scottish and Welsh systems are arguably more sensitive, as discussed below. Government is therefore seeking to treat grant distribution as a control system, but with a methodology rooted in equalisation, and with little of the flexibility such systems need to remain viable.

LESSON 2: SIZE LIMITS SENSITIVITY

18. If improving the sensitivity of the SSA system is an objective, then it is of interest to see how other systems attempt to achieve it. One way is the use of discretion to modify formulae to be more in line with historic spending patterns. But discretion can best be exercised at a local level. The ability to take into account the individual circumstances of LAs and determine priorities depends on good local knowledge. Size is an important constraint. It is therefore no accident that all the equalisation systems considered apart from English SSAs use a two-stage process to determine allocations, with discretion applied at a regional level. In this context, because they cover a small number of LAs, the Scottish and Welsh systems resemble regional systems. It would be difficult to incorporate a discretionary approach within a central system distributing grant to more than 400 LAs.

19. Size also inhibits the consultation process. It is evident that part of the reason for the greater acceptability of the Scottish and Welsh systems to the LAs involved is that LAs feel more part of the negotiation process and better able to influence the outcomes. Virtually all Welsh counties and Scottish regions are represented in the negotiations, and a significant proportion of districts. This allows LAs to be more aware of their respective concerns and problems, and make judgements about the merits of one another's views. It also encourages LAs to make deals, knowing that concessions made today are likely to be repaid tomorrow. In Scotland, the single association, the Convention of Scottish Local Authorities (COSLA) orchestrates this process and seeks to achieve an agreed line before negotiations with the Scottish Office commence. It is likely that, with a strong local authority perspective, this process reinforces empirical methods of distribution based on past expenditure and may therefore be less free of perverse incentives. The process in Scotland and Wales is in contrast to the situation in England, where the LA Associations' primary role in seeking to win more grant for their own member authorities can render the consultation process less productive.

20. The Scottish experience also shows how government could adopt a more 'hands-off' approach to the details of the allocation system. The Scottish Office position is that the chief concern of government is fixing the total amount of GAE and that, within that total, the details of the distribution to LAs are of less significance. It is therefore generally happy to accept COSLA's preferred options for implementing improvements to the allocation process, provided it is satisfied that any changes are fair and equitable between tiers and types of authority.

LESSON 3: DISAGGREGATION IMPROVES SENSITIVITY

21. The systems considered do not provide many hints about the construction of appropriate assessment models, but Scotland and Wales demonstrate some interesting contrasts. Both countries adopt a more disaggregated approach to model building than England, particularly with regard to district-level services. This allows a wider and more relevant range of indicators to be included in the modelling process, and there is evidence that this has significantly increased sensitivity (see Annex to this Appendix).

22. In the Scottish GAE system, services which are difficult to model, or where the costs affect certain LAs disproportionately, are sometimes allocated on the basis of actual or budgeted expenditure (amounting to 12% of district expenditure and 6% of regional expenditure). While this practice can make a real contribution to improving the sensitivity of the allocation process, it must be used appropriately in order to avoid simply rewarding the high spenders, thus providing perverse incentives to LAs. Such a combination of disaggregation, negotiation and reliance on historic expenditure is likely to work better where the number of LAs is low, and would be unlikely to work well for direct allocation to more than 400 LAs.

23. Where a single *primary needs indicator* is found to be satisfactory for a particular service, which is only possible where services are disaggregated, the avoidance of a regression against past expenditure reduces the potential for statistical bias. The potential for feedback is also reduced because LA spending decisions are more variable at a disaggregated level than in total, although the risk of feedback is not removed.

A5. Annex

TO DISAGGREGATE OR NOT TO DISAGGREGATE?
LESSONS FROM THE ALLOCATION OF GRANT AIDED EXPENDITURE IN
SCOTLAND

SUMMARY

When Grant Related Expenditure Assessments (GREs) were replaced in England by Standard Spending Assessments (SSAs) in 1990, the opportunity was taken to reduce the number of assessments from about 60 to 21, to improve the simplicity and the understandability of the system. This change has attracted some criticism, particularly from district councils, whose SSA is now principally determined by just one assessment. They argue that it is now too simple to reflect adequately the wide range of different local circumstances, and hence that some authorities may be significantly disadvantaged. This contrasts with the approaches taken in Wales, and especially in Scotland, where the trend has been to greater disaggregation. The number of assessments used to allocate Scottish Grant Aided Expenditure (GAE) has increased over the years and, for 1993/94, was 100 (24 for district services and 76 for regional services).

This note seeks to assess the value that such extra detail might add to SSAs, by comparing the contrasting approaches in Scotland and England, while recognising that SSAs and GAEs work somewhat differently. It is shown that the most important assessments are those which are large and/or have a distribution markedly different from the population base.

Significant changes in the allocation of GAE to district councils would occur with fewer than eight separate assessments, indicating that disaggregation does play an important role in determining district-level allocations in Scotland. Similar results are shown to be plausible in England, although the balance between sensitivity and administrative burden is of necessity a matter for judgement.

For regional/county-level services, the case for disaggregation is much less clear. Although a few cases are identified where further disaggregation might be beneficial, the general conclusion is that the level of disaggregation employed in England is unlikely to make the allocation significantly less sensitive than in Scotland. The only major exception is the miscellaneous Other Services block, which, for the same reason as that advanced for district services, would benefit from a more disaggregated approach. The case is less compelling, however, because it represents a much smaller proportion of a multi-purpose authority's spending than for shire districts.

INTRODUCTION

1. When Grant Related Expenditure Assessments (GREs) were replaced by Standard Spending Assessments (SSAs) in England in 1990, a key design objective was simplification. The number of assessments was reduced to about a third of the original number, much of this achieved in the Other Services Block, where about 30 assessments were aggregated into two main blocks – District-level services and County-level services (determined by which tier of local government normally provided the service in non-metropolitan areas). This left the majority of a shire district's SSA determined by just one assessment[1].

2. This decision has attracted criticism from local authorities (LAs). Many cannot believe that a formula based solely on the area's density, sparsity and a composite index of social deprivation can properly characterise the spending needs of district councils. There have therefore been calls to revert to the original formulation or at least to split the services up into a number of groups with similar characteristics (disaggregation).

3. Scotland and Wales both use a disaggregated approach for assessing district-level services i.e. each significant service has its own assessment (although in Wales, a blanket adjustment for social deprivation is subsequently applied to the results[2]). This note analyses the Scottish approach to Grant Aided Expenditure (GAE) in order to clarify whether disaggregation appears to lead to a better explanation of differences in local spending in Scotland, and to discover guidelines which could be used to implement the best features of such an approach in England. In making the comparison, it is not assumed that individual GAE assessments are the only, or the best, method available – but their general acceptance in Scotland at least indicates that they are a reasonable reflection of differences in local needs.

HOW GAE IS ALLOCATED TO SCOTTISH DISTRICT COUNCILS

4. There are 53 district councils (and 3 most-purpose Islands councils) in Scotland, providing a similar range of services to those in England, with some exceptions. For example, in Scotland refuse disposal is a district function, whereas electoral registration and the administration of local taxes are carried out at regional level. GAE totals are calculated by the Scottish Office annually for each of 24 services, and these have to be distributed to LAs, taking into account differences in spending needs.

5. Fifteen of the services are distributed initially pro-rata to *primary indicators* (PIs), most of which are some measure of population, adjusted in some cases to reflect the recipients of the service (Table A5.1). Some PIs are measures of the service workload e.g. Crematoria costs are allocated pro-rata to the number of cremations. Seven of the services also use one or more *secondary indicators* (SI) to fine tune the assessment, the weights for these being derived from regression analyses of historic expenditure. The effect of the SI is to redistribute some of the initial allocation by the PI, a different approach to that of SSAs. Eight services which have atypical expenditure patterns and which cannot be represented adequately by PIs and SIs are distributed on the basis of actual or budgeted expenditure.

---

1   *The main elements not covered were Capital Financing (the major item), Rail Support, Flood Defence, Coast Protection and Revenue Interest Receipts*

2   *A description of the Welsh system is given in A Review of SSAs in Wales (Audit Commission), Background Paper 8.6*

48

Table A5.1
METHOD OF ALLOCATION FOR DISTRICT SERVICES

Service	Primary Indicator	Secondary Indicator
Miscellaneous Services	Total Populaion	
Teachers' Remoteness	Total Populaion	
Parks, Allotments & Playing Fields	Adjusted Population (A)	Settlement pattern
Rest of Leisure & Recreation	Adjusted Population (A)	
Refuse Collection	Adjusted Population (B)	Additive sparsity
Street Cleaning	Adjusted Population (B)	Settlement pattern, Area deprivation
Refuse Disposal	Adjusted Population (B)	% waste processed, multiplicative sparsity
Environmental Health	Adjusted Population (B)	Additive sparsity, settlement pattern
Libraries	Adjusted Population (C)	
Sports Facilities & Swimming pools	Sport-weighted population	Unemployment benefit
Burial Grounds	Burial Grounds (ha)	Interments/ha of burial ground
Housing Benefit Admin.	Weighted caseload	
Building Control	No of control warrants	
Homelessness	Homeless households	
Crematoria	No of cremations	

Allocated via actual/budgeted expenditure

Planning & Economic Development	—
Museums & Art Galleries	—
Non-Road Lighting	—
Housing Improvement Grants	—
Tourism	—
District Courts	—
Public Analyst	—
Trading Services	—

Allocated via special formula

Non-Domestic Rating Adjustment	—

Note: Adjusted populations (A), (B), (C) are different weighted combinations of resident population, commuters and tourist bed-nights

MEASURING THE SENSITIVITY OF THE ALLOCATION

6. The use of individual assessments for each service should make the allocation sensitive to the local circumstances of each LA. But having separate assessments for two different services may make little difference to the final allocation of GAE if the pattern of distribution is similar or if the total amount of GAE for the services is relatively small. The impact of each service on the sensitivity of the allocation process can be measured by calculating, for each district, the change in its GAE if that service were distributed on a simple per capita basis and then finding the average and the maximum (absolute) % difference over all districts. These calculations can also be applied to estimate the impact of groups of services, according to their method of

49

Exhibit A5.2

CONTRIBUTIONS TO THE SENSITIVITY OF THE 1993-94 GAE ALLOCATION

The impact of each service, and group of services, on the sensitivity of the allocation process can be measured.

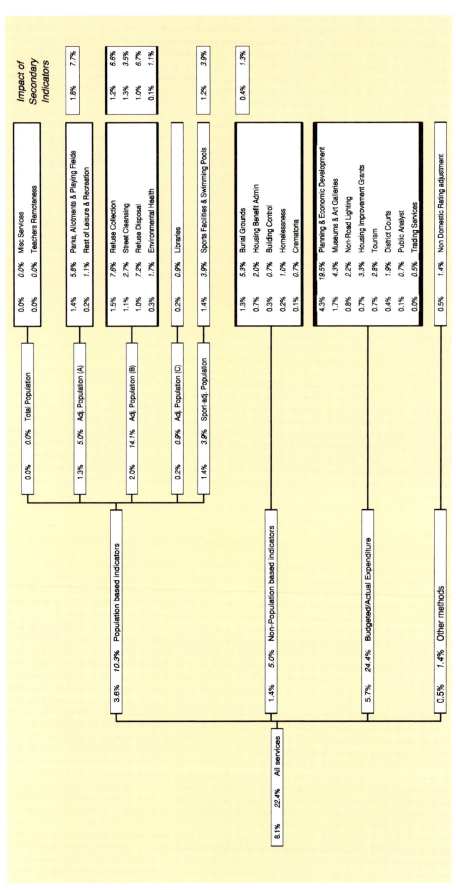

Notes: 1 The data shown against each service or group is a measure of its contribution to the sensitivity of the assessment calculated by working out the difference between the actual distribution and ore based on total population alone

2 The figures shown are the absolute percentage differences, averaged over all districts (maximum in italics)

3 The final column shows the marginal impact of secondary indicators, where used, also in terms of absolute percentage differences

50

allocation, and the marginal impact of SIs[1] (Exhibit A5.2). Overall, a per capita distribution would change allocations by 8% on average, up to a maximum of 22%.

7. The analysis demonstrates that services vary markedly in their impact on sensitivity. Planning & Economic Development has easily the biggest effect (an average difference of 4% and a maximum of 20%), while at the other end of the scale, a number of services made very little difference overall (Exhibit A5.3).

Exhibit A5.3
CONTRIBUTION TO ASSESSMENT SENSITIVITY
Some services are much more important for assessment sensitivity than others.

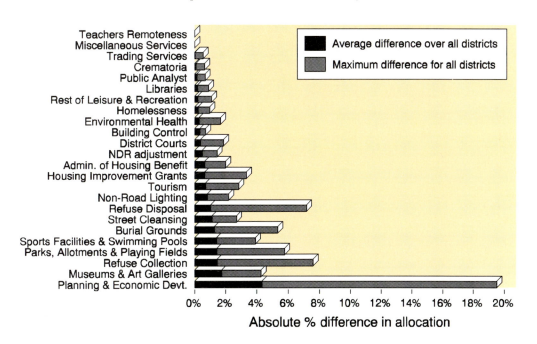

Note: Data shown is the difference between the actual allocation and a per capita distribution

8. The identification of an order of importance for sensitivity allows an evaluation to be made of the benefits of disaggregation. Starting with a per-capita distribution for every service, the actual distribution for individual services can be introduced in turn in their order of importance. With fewer than 9 assessments, some districts experience changes in allocation of over 10% (Exhibit A5.4, overleaf). However, the marginal impact of a greater number of separate assessments soon diminishes. There is no 'right' level of disaggregation, but the analysis does serve to demonstrate two things:

(a)   having a number of separate assessments does make a difference to the final allocation;

(b)   some services could be grouped together and distributed on a per capita basis without making much difference.

---

1   *Prior to analysis, the data was adjusted for Libraries and Building Control, because these are carried out by the region rather than the district in 3 cases*

Exhibit A5.4
DISAGGREGATION AND SENSITIVITY
With fewer than 9 assessments, some districts experience changes in allocation of over 10%

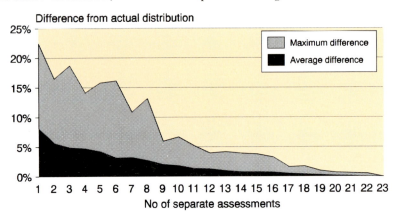

9. This argument alone is not sufficient to show that disaggregation is beneficial, because it is based solely on a comparison with a per capita distribution. It may be that the number of assessments could be lower than that indicated by the analysis because some services with similar distributions could be grouped together. In practice, there is little scope for such groupings because the distributions of the eight most significant services do not display any marked similarities with each other. This suggests that no simple formula of the type used in England would be able to replicate the GAE allocations, and gives grounds for thinking that disaggregation may indeed be beneficial for district-level SSAs.

ESTABLISHING GUIDELINES FOR DISAGGREGATION

10. Why should different services be more important to allocate individually than others ? Some general principles can be identified (Exhibit A5.5). The more important services are those which have one or more of the following characteristics:

(a)   large or medium-sized expenditure;

(b)   allocated via a secondary indicator, or by actual/budget expenditure, or by a non-population based primary indicator.

11. The message of this analysis is clear. The most important contributions to sensitivity are from services which have a distribution pattern significantly different from the population base and/or account for relatively high levels of expenditure. These principles can be applied to the English context to get a feel for how disaggregation might improve the sensitivity of the allocation. (This is preferable to assuming that the same services would be the most important in England, because of differences in definition and in the nature of the services in the two countries).

APPLYING THE LESSONS TO ENGLAND

12. The size of services is obtainable from historic expenditure data. Differences in expenditure patterns can be inferred from an analysis of correlations of service expenditures (Exhibit A5.6). Three groups of services can be identified:

Exhibit A5.5

REASONS FOR DIFFERENCES IN ALLOCATION SENSITIVITY

Services (Decreasing in Importance)	Impact on sensitivity Average	Impact on sensitivity Maximum	Allocation Method Primary Indicator Type	Allocation Method Secondary Indicator? (Yes/No)	Average Budget (£s per head)
Planning & Economic Devt.	4.3%	19.5%	-	N	
Museums & Art Galleries	1.7%	4.3%	-	N	
Refuse Collection	1.5%	7.6%	P	Y	
Parks, Alls. & Playing Fields	1.4%	5.8%	P	Y	
Sports Facs. & Swimming Pools	1.4%	3.9%	P	Y	
Burial Grounds	1.3%	5.3%	N	Y	
Street Cleansing	1.1%	2.7%	P	Y	
Refuse Disposal	1.0%	7.2%	P	Y	
Non-Road Lighting	0.8%	2.2%	-	N	
Tourism	0.7%	2.8%	-	N	
Housing Improvement Grants	0.7%	3.3%	-	N	
Admin. of Housing Benefit	0.7%	2.0%	N	N	
NDR adjustment	0.5%	1.4%	-	N	
District Courts	0.4%	1.9%	-	N	
Building Control	0.3%	0.7%	N	N	
Environmental Health	0.3%	1.7%	P	Y	
Homelessness	0.2%	1.0%	N	N	
Rest of Leisure & Recreation	0.2%	1.1%	P	N	
Libraries	0.2%	0.9%	P	N	
Public Analyst	0.1%	0.7%	-	N	
Crematoria	0.1%	0.7%	N	N	
Trading Services	0.0%	0.5%	-	N	
Miscellaneous Services	0.0%	0.0%	P	N	
Teachers Remoteness	0.0%	0.0%	P	N	

(Average Budget axis scale: 0, 5, 10, 15, 20, 25)

Comments

a The highest contributions are from
b services with large or medium budgets
c and which are allocated either:
d - via secondary indicators (c-h)
e - or via actual/budget expenditure (a,b)
f
g
h
i The next most important group are
j services with small budgets which are
k allocated either:
l - via actual/budget expenditure (i-k,m-n)
m - or via non-population based primary
n indicators (l,o)
o
p The least important group are services
q which either:
r - have very small budgets (q,t-v,x)
s - or are allocated via population based
t primary indicators (r,s,w)
u
v The exception is p (Env. Health), which
w has both a medium-sized budget and is
x allocated via (2) secondary indicators.
   This is because the weightings of the
   secondary indicators are small compared
   to the primary indicator

Notes 1 The contribution to sensitivity of each service is measured as the difference between the actual allocation of GAE and a simple per capita distribution, and expressed as a percentage difference

2 The primary indicator types are:
    P Population-based
    N Non-population based e.g. workload
    - Not applicable (e.g. distributed via actual/budget expenditure)

(a)   A large group of 11 services all with high inter-correlations

(b)   A second group of 3 services with poor inter-correlations but reasonably strongly correlated with the first group

(c)   A third group of 4 services with no strong correlations with any other service.

13. The first group contains services where expenditure is broadly in line with population. Candidates for separate assessment are therefore likely to come from the larger services within each group, but with size being less important in the second and third groups due to their atypical distributions (Table A5.2).

14. The number of services selected is a matter for discretion, depending on the balance sought between sensitivity and the administrative effort associated with a higher number of assessments. It will also depend on whether appropriate indicators can be found for distributing each service and whether these imply allocations which are different enough to make a separate assessment worthwhile.

Table A5.2
IDENTIFYING CANDIDATES FOR SEPARATE ASSESSMENT IN ENGLAND

Service	Spending 1986/87 (£m)	Spending As abs %	Most important services	
			Due to size	Due to spending pattern
Recreation	481.1	28.8%	*	
Refuse collection	254.6	15.2%	*	
Environmental health	209.5	12.5%	*	
Other services	190.7	11.4%		
Local tax collection	92.8	5.6%		
Concessionary fares	66.1	4.0%		
Rent allowances	52.6	3.1%		
Local tax rebates	41.6	2.5%		
Museums	40.1	2.4%		
Electoral registration	16.4	1.0%		
Allotments	2.4	0.1%		
Parking	-35.9	2.1%		*
Cemeteries	21.3	1.3%		
Non-HRA housing	9.2	0.6%		
Planning control	118.2	7.1%		*
Planning implementation	22.3	1.3%		*
Building regulations	15.3	0.9%		
Economic development	-0.7	0.0%		

As it happens, the services indicated from this analysis are broadly in line with those appearing to be most important in Scotland, bearing in mind differences in responsibilities.

15. Different types of assessments might arise because of differences in approach in the two countries. For example, in Scotland, considerable use is made of actual/budget expenditure, which has been avoided where possible in England because of the potential for abuse. This does not

Exhibit A5.6

CORRELATION MATRIX FOR THE OTHER DISTRICT SERVICE EXPENDITURE

Most services are quite highly correlated, but some exhibit very individual patterns of expenditure.

	Resident Population	1	2	3	4	5	6	7	8	9	10	11	12	13	14	15	16	17	18
1 Rate Rebates	.70																		
2 Other Services	.61	.48																	
3 Environmental Health	.80	.65	.72																
4 Rent Allowances	.73	.70	.64	.79															
5 Electoral Registration	.73	.52	.55	.66	.70														
6 Rate Collection	.84	.68	.68	.78	.76	.75													
7 Refuse Collection	.88	.73	.56	.76	.71	.69	.80												
8 Recreation	.79	.74	.70	.80	.73	.62	.78	.80											
9 Museums	.70	.60	.53	.72	.66	.54	.65	.68	.69										
10 Allotments	.45	.46	.47	.61	.52	.41	.52	.48	.59	.54									
11 Concessionary Fares	.51	.49	.49	.55	.47	.30	.53	.48	.68	.58	.46								
12 Cemeteries	.45	.45	.37	.52	.42	.27	.45	.47	.50	.46	.52	.35							
13 Parking	.43	.27	.46	.53	.52	.40	.41	.37	.36	.38	.35	.31	.18						
14 Non-HRA Housing	.34	.34	.39	.37	.41	.36	.46	.36	.39	.35	.25	.21	.28	.08					
15 Planning Control	.35	.25	.18	.31	.26	.30	.36	.33	.19	.24	.15	.13	.23	.10	.29				
16 Planning Implementation	.04	.08	.00	.04	.02	.01	.02	.03	.05	.09	.09	.13	.15	.03	.08	.44			
17 Building Regulations	.19	.11	.18	.24	.21	.11	.22	.19	.19	.11	.10	.11	.12	.00	.13	.29	.02		
18 Economic Development	.11	.03	.28	.20	.29	.23	.23	.02	.17	.05	.28	.11	.08	.14	.23	.18	.04	.06	

Note: *Data is 1986-87 outturn expenditure for shire districts*
Source: *DoE*

imply that alternative satisfactory assessments cannot be found. In the previous GRE system, indicators such as planning applications were used for Planning Control and unemployment for Economic Development.

REGIONAL SERVICES

16. Regional services in Scotland are also considerably more disaggregated than their SSA equivalents. While English counties have 20 assessments, covering Education, Social Services, Highway Maintenance, Fire & Civil Defence, Police, and Other County Services, Scottish Regions have 76, nearly four times as many (Table A5.3). Although the difference is not as marked as for district services, it is large enough to suggest a significantly different approach. As before, the key question is whether the extra detail leads to additional sensitivity.

Table A5.3
ASSESSMENTS FOR REGIONAL SERVICES

	Number
Education	15
Social Services	22
Roads & Transport	8
Police	7
Fire	3
Other Services	21
Total	76

17. The reason for the greater number of assessments in Scotland is illustrated by an analysis of the Education service. In England there are 5 assessments, classified by age group: Under 5, Primary, Secondary, Post-16 and Other Educational Services. All costs relating to the age-group are contained within the relevant assessment. In Scotland, there are 15 assessments, categorised in terms of activity types e.g. teaching, transport, non-teaching costs & property, bursaries (Exhibit A5.7). Only teaching costs are split by age group (nursery, primary, secondary, special), because it accounts for over 50% of the total.

18. Over 80% of total Education GAE relates to just three of the categories (primary teaching; secondary teaching; and non-teaching staff and property), each of which accounts for over 20% of the total. After these, the next largest category (Community Education) accounts for less than 4%. All three major categories are allocated via pupil numbers, and with no SI in the case of Secondary Teaching. Following the guidelines identified earlier, the smaller categories of cost are only likely to be worth distributing separately if their distribution pattern is markedly different from population.

19. An analysis similar to that done for district services can identify the contribution to sensitivity of each category. Apart from the three larger categories, the most important contributions are from school transport, teachers for deprivation and Further Education travel & bursaries (Table A5.4). These six categories appear to provide the bulk of the allocation sensitivity, but it could be argued that, of the smaller assessments, only School Transport makes enough of a difference to justify considering a separate SSA.

Exhibit A5.7

ALLOCATION OF GAE FOR EDUCATION SERVICES

Cost Type		ALLOCATION METHOD		GAE	GAE	Difference Measure*	
		PI	SI(s)	£	% total	Av.	Max
School teachers	Secondary Teaching	Secondary pupils		616,817	27.7%	1.7%	5.5%
	Primary Teaching	Primary pupils	% pupils in small rural schools	494,713	22.2%	1.4%	4.1%
	Special School teaching	Population 5-15		74,727	3.4%	0.1%	0.4%
	Nursery Teaching	Population 3-4		19,335	0.9%	0.0%	0.1%
Pupil-related costs	Non-teaching staff & property	Pupils (inc adults)	Urban settlement pattern/NDR adjustment	726,530	32.6%	2.1%	4.3%
	School Transport	Pupils (ex adults)	Rural settlement pattern	39,939	1.8%	1.2%	2.6%
	Hostels and clothing	Pupils (ex adults)	Hostel places/1000 pupils,Inc.Suppt. recipients	20,575	0.9%	0.3%	0.8%
Costs related to	Community Education	Total population		87,687	3.9%	0.0%	0.0%
other indicators	School meals	Pupil meals	Income Support recipients	39,786	1.8%	0.3%	0.6%
	Residual Further Education	Population over 16		25,357	1.1%	0.0%	0.0%
Costs allocated	FE: Travel /Bursaries	—		43,914	2.0%	0.5%	1.4%
by budget/actuals	Teachers for deprivation	—		24,734	1.1%	0.8%	1.2%
etc.	School Bursaries	—		4,826	0.2%	0.1%	0.2%
	Teachers for ethnic minorities	—		4,801	0.2%	0.1%	0.1%
	Gaelic	—		2,288	0.1%	0.1%	0.4%
	Total			2,226,028	100.0%	5.3%	16.6%

Note: Difference measure is the average percentage difference in total allocation resulting from per capita allocation of the given category (excludes Island councils)

57

Table A5.4
CONTRIBUTIONS TO ALLOCATION SENSITIVITY OF THE SCOTTISH EDUCATION GAE

Category	Impact on allocation (%)	
	Average	**Maximum**
Non-teaching staff & property	2.1%	4.3%
Secondary Teaching	1.7%	5.5%
Primary Teaching	1.4%	4.1%
School Transport	1.2%	2.6%
Teachers for deprivation	0.8%	1.2%
FE: Travel/Bursaries	0.5%	1.4%

20. SSAs are distributed in England within each age group in relation to pupil or population numbers, with additional indicators to take account of sparsity, free school meals and additional educational needs, a composite indicator relating to social deprivation. The relative merits of the different indicators used in England and Scotland, and whether services are better classified by age group or by type of activity, are debatable. But in terms of the level of disaggregation, it would be difficult to argue that SSAs are significantly less sensitive than GAEs.

21. A comparison of Social Services GAEs with SSAs reveals a broadly similar pattern. GAEs are more evenly distributed than for Education, with the largest 6 of the 21 categories accounting for 65% of the total (Exhibit A5.8). Two of these (Handicapped: Operational, Other Services: Operational) are distributed by population, but the others are based on SIs and their distributions therefore exhibit average differences from a per capita allocation in the range 1.5%-3.2% (maximum differences tend to be about 2 or 3 times the average). These are arguably large enough to warrant separate treatment. Of the remaining categories, there are only 4 possible candidates for disaggregation (Table A5.5). Thus at most 10 categories would be sufficient to avoid any significant loss in sensitivity.

Table A5.5
CONTRIBUTIONS TO ALLOCATION SENSITIVITY OF THE SOCIAL SERVICES GAE

Category	Impact on allocation (%)	
	Average	**Maximum**
Residential school pupils	1.5%	3.2%
Children's day care	1.4%	3.2%
Community Care: DSS transfer	1.1%	3.9%
AIDS (Operational)	0.9%	2.4%

22. In comparison, there are 4 SSA assessments for Social Services (Children, Elderly Domiciliary, Elderly Residential and Other Services), which employ social indicators and age weightings, as for GAEs. The main difference from the GAE distribution is the more disaggregated approach to children's services, which account for 4 of the 10 most important categories identified above. If the Children's GAE were allocated in line with the largest category (Community & Residential Care), the change in allocation would average 2.5%, with a maximum difference of 5%. Whether this is acceptable is a matter for judgement, but the level of disaggregation employed in England would not be responsible for a significant loss in sensitivity.

Exhibit A5.8
SOCIAL SERVICE GAE ALLOCATION
The largest 6 of the 21 categories account for 65% of the total.

Client Group	Category	GAE £	GAE %	Difference measure*	Method of Allocation: PI	SI
Elderly	Domiciliary	117,825	15.7%	2.0%	Weighted Populn 65+	Low Income Pensioners
	Residential	89,418	11.9%	3.2%	Weighted Populn 75+	% of 75+ populn who are 80+
	Admin	28,936	3.9%	0.4%	Elderly GAEs	
Children	Community & Resid. Care	74,561	10.0%	1.5%	Populn Under 16	Children Of People On Income Support
	Admin	68,724	9.2%	2.3%	Children's GAEs	
	Day Care	30,370	4.1%	1.4%	Population Under 5	Single Parents With Children Under 5
	Residential Schools	20,480	2.7%	1.5%	Resid. School Pupils	
	Panels	6,899	0.9%	0.3%	Referrals	
AIDS	Operational	6,645	0.9%	0.9%	Weighted AIDS/HIV Cases	
	Admin	181	0.0%	0.0%	Weighted AIDS/HIV Cases	
Handicapped	Operational	70,208	9.4%	0.2%	Populn 16-64	
	Admin	14,468	1.9%	0.0%	Populn 16-64	
	Independent Living Fund	2,800	0.4%	0.0%	Populn 16-64	
Other Services	Operational	65,353	8.7%	0.0%	Total Population	
	Admin	20,617	2.8%	0.0%	Total Population	
Community Care	DSS Transfer	40,600	5.4%	1.1%	Elderly/Handicapped GAEs	Transitional Adjustment
	Implementation	20,000	2.7%	0.2%	Elderly/Handicapped GAEs	
	Assessment & Care Mgt.	8,900	1.2%	0.0%	Populn 16-64	
	Mental Illness	7,400	1.0%	0.2%	Specific Grant	
	Other Developments	4,100	0.5%	0.0%	Total Population	
	Inspection & Registration	2,000	0.3%	0.1%	Elderly Residential GAEs	
General	Admin	47,926	6.4%	0.5%	Social Work GAEs	
		748,411	100.0%	7.7%		

Note: Difference measure is the *average percentage difference in total allocation resulting from per capita allocation of the given category (excludes Island councils)*

23. The results of similar analyses on other regional service areas are likely to be similar, except in the case of the 'Other Services' group, which in England is represented by a single assessment. The same argument that was presented for district services would suggest that some measure of disaggregation would be desirable. The only other potential candidate is the Police service, which is represented by a single assessment in England, but by seven in Scotland. Analysis shows that there might be merit in separate assessment for Rent Allowances, Pensions and Administration, but differences in the services may mean that this conclusion does not follow for England (Exhibit A5.9).

Exhibit A5.9

POLICE GAE ALLOCATION

	GAE £m	GAE %	Difference measure Av.	Difference measure Max.	Method of Allocation PI	SI
Staff	386,816	73.6%	0.0%	0.0%	Standard Establishment	
Pensions	51,113	9.7%	1.4%	2.9%	Standard Establishment	Standard Establishment/station
Rent Allowances	45,716	8.7%	2.1%	5.1%	Standard Establishment	Settlement Pattern
Property	20,320	3.9%	0.6%	1.1%	—	(actual expenditure)
Admin	12,871	2.4%	1.1%	3.5%	Standard Establishment	Settlement Pattern
Transport	8,562	1.6%	0.2%	0.5%	—	(actual expenditure)
Travel Warrants	176	0.0%	0.1%	0.5%	—	(budget)
	525,574	100%	1.6%	3.7%		

Note: *Difference measure is the percentage difference in total allocation resulting from allocation of the given category pro rata to std. establishment (excludes Island councils)*

61

Appendix 6

VARIATIONS ON A THEME: A COMPARISON OF SSAs WITH RESOURCE ALLOCATION SYSTEMS IN EUROPE

INTRODUCTION

1. The Audit Commission commissioned Glen Bramley to undertake a modest comparative review of systems equivalent to SSAs in a number of European countries. This appendix is a summary of the main conclusions of the work. The main report is also being made available as a Background Paper to the main publications (see Appendix 8).

2. The report provides a description of the systems of local government finance and grants in six European (EC) countries. The information and comments are structured around a checklist of issues, and are based upon both published material and the comments of expert informants contacted in each country. The countries covered were: Denmark, Netherlands, Germany, France, Italy, Portugal. These together with Britain fairly well represent the range of experience within the Community. Annex 1 at the end of the report provides background information in tabular form on some of the key facts about local government systems and finance in these countries. Annex 2 lists the key informants who helped with the study; the Commission is very appreciative of the time and effort put in by these individuals over a very short timescale. Annex 3 provides a bibliography, including the published studies referred to in this report. Earlier comparative studies have been particularly helpful, including the work of Coopers and Lybrand (1990b) for the Joseph Rowntree Foundation and the Council of Europe's work steered by Philip Blair.

DIFFERING CONTEXTS: SCOPE AND FINANCING OF LOCAL GOVERNMENT

3. The size and scope of local government varies enormously (see Table A6.1). Scandinavia, especially Denmark, stands out by assigning large parts of a well-developed welfare state (including education and health) to the local government level. Britain and the Netherlands are intermediate, with quite substantial local government sectors. The other three major EC countries all have relatively smaller local sectors, but in these cases regional authorities take substantial responsibilities. The share of local expenditure and functions is generally either static or growing. Local authorities, except in the major cities, tend to be much smaller, although two-tier systems are typical. Social services are less developed within local government in some countries, while in Portugal local government is a relatively recent creation. The common core of services nearly always provided by local government includes: local roads and transport, planning, refuse, leisure and culture.

Table A6.1
THE SIZE AND FINANCING OF LOCAL GOVERNMENT EXPENDITURE

	Net expenditure as % of GDP		Grants as % of net expenditure	
	1981	1987	1981	1991
United Kingdom	10.5	11.6	61	82
Denmark	30.0	24.2	43	29
Netherlands	11.3	17.6	94	90
Germany	5.6	5.7	47	45
France	4.5	5.7*	39	36
Italy	5.9	5.0	95	88
Portugal	2.9	4.0	81	61

*Note: * France: municipalities only (9.3% inc. Regions & Depts)*
Sources: Council of Europe (1986), Coopers and Lybrand Deloitte (1990b), key informants.

4. Table 1 also shows the proportion of net expenditure financed by grants (precise comparisons are difficult due to definitional problems). The recent increase in the share of grants in Britain goes rather against the trend in Europe, although it can be seen that some countries have even higher shares of grant and even less reliance on local taxes. Conversely, it is clearly possible to operate local government with a much higher share of local taxation than in Britain.

CONTROL AND MONEY

5. The systems described are quite a mixture. Some are systems for distributing money with at least partial or crude equalization objectives, in a context where local government has considerable independent sources of revenue. Some are systems for both allocating money and exerting strong control, by virtue of the relative lack of local revenue sources. In this group of countries we do not find systems of control without money, that is, controls over local revenue raising. However, examples of this are to be found in Europe, for example Sweden, which recently imposed a temporary freeze on local tax rates.

6. On the whole, in the countries studied we do not find central governments taking such a strong stance on the control of local expenditure and taxation as is currently found in Britain. This seems to reflect a widespread sentiment in favour of decentralisation and local democracy. There seems to be more tolerance of local diversity in service provision. In addition, political systems often seem to give considerable weight to local interests in national policy forums. Nevertheless, in a number of cases, central government clearly does show some concern about local tax rates.

7. In addition, the control totals for grants and assigned revenues often build in an automatic link with the revenue of major national taxes. This gives local government revenue a greater natural buoyancy at the cost of some pro-cyclical fluctuation. It means that the general presumption is normally that local government shall share in the national prosperity to the same degree that central government does. This seems to place central-local relations on a rather different plane to that found in Britain, where central government attempts to use its discretion to impose different targets on local government from those applied to its own operations.

EQUALIZATION

8. In all of the countries studied, and across Europe more generally, equalization is quite an important goal in the systems of local government finance. Its importance seems to be growing over time, partly as a consequence of attempts to consolidate myriad specific grants into broader block grants. Equalization is more fully developed in countries where the system of local government is more mature and extensive, particularly in northern Europe.

9. Resource equalization seems to be more important and to receive more attention than needs equalization in a number of cases. This is partly because specific grants often play more of an implicit role in compensating for differences in needs. It seems that the connections between needs and resource equalization are important and would repay closer examination. Areas which are relatively poor and deprived could gain more through resource equalization mechanisms than they might through the kinds of needs formulae found in Europe. In the British context, the concern expressed about the lack of economic variables in SSA might be mitigated if there were more attention given to resources. Conversely, the concerns of cities might be less if they retained access to a not fully equalized business tax base.

10. None of the countries studied have systems which could be described as providing for full equalization in the sense in which this is understood in Britain. There does not seem to be strong pressure to equalize fully and this seems to go along with a tolerance of and respect for local diversity.

THE NATURE OF GRANT FORMULAE

11. The needs and grant formulae found in Europe seem to give most emphasis to basic demographic and physical features of areas. Much less attention is given to social characteristics. This reflects in part the service responsibilities of local government and perhaps the more extreme variation in physical conditions between often very small authorities. Specific grants may be used to respond to social problems.

12. Grant formulae are generally simpler than in Britain, with more transparency and recognition of rough justice. They also seem to be less controversial. On the whole, service standards are not generally spelt out in detail and do not provide a basis for grant calculation, at least as far as general grants are concerned.

13. Considerable parts of the overall grant amounts, in all cases except Portugal, could be described as matching or related in some way to output, expenditure or effort. This may be contrasted with the British case, where the main grant since 1990 has been a fixed lump sum grant. The idea that authorities should not necessarily be grant aided for services which they do not provide finds considerable support in Europe. However, there is no very clear pattern of exactly which activities should be specific-grant aided.

14. The idea that grants should take the existing pattern of expenditure as a starting point and not disrupt the historical inheritance too sharply is quite widely respected. This can operate both directly and indirectly, through the research procedures underlying grant formulae. However, the formalized, systematic and periodically updated use of regression analysis, which characterizes the British system, is not found in the same form in these European cases. In general, large city authorities have much higher per capita expenditures and tend to receive correspondingly higher levels of grant.

PROCESS ISSUES

15. There seems to be much more consensus and much less conflict in central-local relations on the European mainland. There are a number of possible reasons for this. The more positive sentiments towards decentralisation and localism have already been mentioned. In some countries (France and Italy for example) the close connection between local and national political elites is frequently remarked upon. This may be institutionalised in overlapping functions and partnership approaches, often involving regional authorities. Another important factor must surely be that in most of these countries national governments are coalitions arising out of proportional representation systems.

16. National ministers may be less tempted to manipulate general grant formulae because they have more alternative levers through which to exercise their discretion in the form of specific grants.

17. Local government collectively often has more institutional influence over the system. For example, in Denmark, the local authority associations have to be consulted about any new service responsibilities and negotiate an agreed figure for the cost involved. These associations also have an influence on the grant mechanics and formula, and this is backed up by their having a very well-established research capability. In Germany, most detailed decisions about grant distribution are made at the Lander (regional) level, where local perspectives are likely to be more influential. In France, the leading role in the distribution of grants is given to a 'Local Finance Committee', composed mainly of local elected politicians.

Appendix 7

FAIR DINKUM? THE AUSTRALIAN GRANTS DISTRIBUTION SYSTEM

PREFACE

This appendix describes the Australian grants system. The Commission always endeavours to compare British local government systems with appropriate international comparisons, but it is unusual for the Commission to search as far as Australia for comparators.

Australia was examined as a consequence of the nature of its grant distribution system. Whilst other European countries have systems to redistribute tax revenue between tiers of local government, none possesses the sophistication of the British model. If anything, the Australian model is more complicated than British counterparts and the process of grant negotiation possesses features which are different from Britain but which could be considered here.

The Australian system is removed from the political arena through the appointment of independent Grants Commissions. Their remit, considerations and conclusions are transparent to all interested parties. In essence, the Australian system of grant allocation is a relatively pure 'expert' system operating independently from mainstream political processes. The establishment of similar independent commissions in Britain could be a possible recommendation of the Audit Commission and it was therefore judged appropriate to assess the characteristics of the Australian model.

Whenever the Commission reviews a process it attempts to view it from the perspective of all interested parties. Therefore visits were made to all three tiers of Australian Government – local councils, states, and the Commonwealth government, as well as to the agencies involved in the grants process. The Annex lists all the bodies visited. The Commission is indebted for the time which they afforded to the study. This report sets out the findings of the work from a British perspective. It does not presume to consider whether the Australian system remains appropriate for current Australian conditions, but does attempt to assess whether Britain can learn useful lessons from the Australian experience. The views in the paper are solely those of the Audit Commission.

STRUCTURE

1. The Australian system cannot be properly understood outside its constitutional context. Unlike British local government, Australian states are governments in their own right protected in their existence by the Australian Federal Constitution of 1901. Whilst central government in Britain regards the grants distribution system to local government as the distribution of central government monies to councils to provide national services, Australian states are quite clear that the monies which the Commonwealth government disburses are state monies collected on their behalf by the Commonwealth government. Up until 1942 the states applied their own income tax, surrendering that power only in wartime emergency conditions. They regard the distribution of Commonwealth grant as simply returning to them their income tax revenues over which the Commonwealth government took stewardship in 1942.

THE COMMONWEALTH GRANTS COMMISSION

2. The Commonwealth Grants Commission is an independent commission appointed to recommend the basis for the distribution of Commonwealth resources to states. It is quite a substantial organisation, employing about 50 staff, and entertaining an involved system of consultation. It was founded in 1933, but in its early decades it mainly arbitrated over special pleading claims; only in the last decade has it developed an Australia-wide formula system. Additionally, in each Australian state there is a state appointed commission which recommends the basis for the distribution of Commonwealth grants earmarked for local government (Exhibit A7.1). Given the political controversy which frequently surrounds the British grant distribution system, the Australian system of appointing a non-political commission to oversee the process bears examination as a possible improvement on the British system.

3. In interpreting its remit the Commonwealth Grants Commission considers both the expenditure requirements of states and their revenue raising capacities. The objective is to provide each state with equivalent capability. In doing so, the Commission assesses standard levels of expenditure and tax raising capability for each appropriate budget element. Australians are quite clear that no externally set standard of services or level of taxation is pre-supposed. Rather, standards are based on an averaging of the actual policies of the states. The Grants Commission compares states with each other on the assumption that each state adopts the same tax raising and expenditure policies which in practice are the Australian-wide average. This does not mean that each state is expected to pursue identical policies but rather that the objective of Common-wealth subsidies is to equip states equally to develop their own state policies. The system is concerned with equalising capability rather than practice.

4. The mechanism for the assessment of grants is simple in concept but complex in practice (Box A7.A, overleaf). In interpreting its remit the Commonwealth Grants Commission holds quinquennial reviews into its methodology and is open annually to representations on how to deal with changing circumstances. Representations are common.

STATE GRANTS COMMISSIONS

5. State Grants Commissions are lesser cousins of the Commonwealth Grants Commission but follow similar principles, albeit to slightly different methodologies. Queensland operates the 'balanced budget' approach, constructing notional budgets for each council and then distributing

Exhibit A7.1

THE STRUCTURE OF THE AUSTRALIAN SYSTEM

The Commonwealth Grants Commission recommends the basis for grants to be distributed to the states and in each state there is a state appointed commission to distribute grant between local authorities.

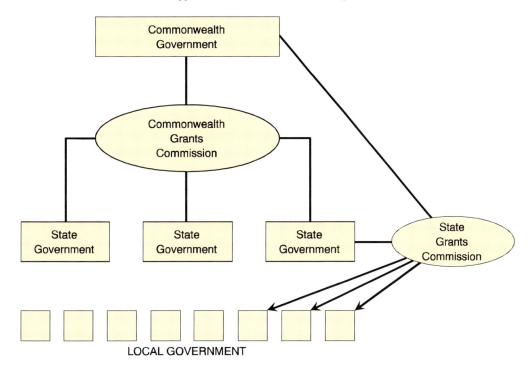

Source: Audit Commission

the available grant according to the notional deficit. (Exhibit A7.2 – overleaf). The other states operate the 'direct assessment technique' constructing indices of unsatisfied expenditure need as the basis for grant distribution. No two states have the exact same formulae even though they may use similar methodology. South Australia has also decided to adopt the 'balanced budget' approach but has yet to implement its decision.

PROCESS

6. Two concepts, implicit in British arrangements are explicitly argued in negotiations between the State and the Commonwealth:

(a) Vertical fiscal imbalance – refers to the differences between own source revenue and own purpose expenditure commitments for a level of government (Exhibit A 7.3 – overleaf). In practice, it means that the Commonwealth raises more tax than its functions require, whilst the States have more functions than their revenue can support. Therefore fiscal balance must be restored through a grants process.

(b) Horizontal fiscal equalisation – a process which 'should enable each state to provide, without having to impose taxes or charges at levels appreciably different from the levels imposed in other states, government services at standards not appreciably different from the standards provided by other states'. Consequently, grants will be differentially awarded to remedy differences in needs and resources amongst the States.

Box A7.A
COMMONWEALTH GRANTS COMMISSION: EQUALISATION IN PRACTICE

(i) The starting point for the assessment of relativities is a detailed analysis of State budgets. Expenditures are classified by functional category and, as far as possible, adjusted to consistent definitions. (Hospitals, police and agricultural services are examples of categories.) From these figures, *standard* expenditures (the population-weighted average of expenditures by the States) are calculated for each category. Similar processes are carried out on the revenue side.

(ii) These standard figures form the basis of all subsequent assessments and calculations. In devising them, the Commission is concerned with what the States usually spend (or raise), not with what they 'should' spend (in whatever sense of that word).

(iii) However, the subsequent equalisation process does require judgements about disabilities. A *disability* is any influence beyond a State's control that requires it to spend more than other States to achieve the same objective, or which requires it to maintain a higher than average burden of taxes in order to raise the same per capita tax revenue. For example, a relatively large number of children in the age group 6-11 in a State would mean greater needs in the provision of primary education; a relatively large number of aged persons or socially disadvantaged groups in a State would mean greater needs in the provision of community health services; and a State economy with a relatively large small business sector will have a disability in raising pay-roll tax.

(iv) Wherever possible, disabilities are measured from objective data, much of which comes from the Australian Bureau of Statistics (census figures, for example). However, there are elements of judgement in deciding what particular influences are beyond the control of the States, and sometimes in the measurements themselves. In general, the Commission assesses the disabilities where it is convinced they exist and where it is able to obtain a sufficiently policy-neutral measure of them.

(v) For each expenditure category, all relevant disabilities are taken into account to determine *standardised expenditure* – that is, the amount a State would need to spend to provide the same level of service at the same level of efficiency as the other States on average. On the other side of the budget, *standardised revenue* is the revenue a State would collect if, given the size of its revenue base, it made an average effort to raise revenue (effort being indicated, for example, by rates and coverage of taxes). The difference between a State's standardised expenditure (or revenue) and the related standard figure is the effect of disabilities.

(vi) Subtracting a State's total standardised revenue from its total standardised expenditure and adjusting the result for the standard, or average, budget result (deficit or surplus) gives a measure of the State's total requirement for assistance from the Commonwealth. Relativities appropriate for the distribution of general revenue assistance are calculated by converting those requirements, after taking account of Commonwealth specific purpose payments received, to per capita terms and expressing them as a proportion of the Victorian figure (Victoria's relativity is 1.000)[1].

Source: Commonwealth Grants Commission, Review of States and Territories General Revenue Grant Relativities: Discussion Paper, Nov. 1991

1   *In future, the presentation of per capita relativities will be based on the Australian average rather than Victoria having a value of 1.000*

70

Exhibit A7.2
QUEENSLAND'S BALANCED BUDGET APPROACH
Queensland constructs notional budgets for each council and then distributes the available grant
according to the notional deficit

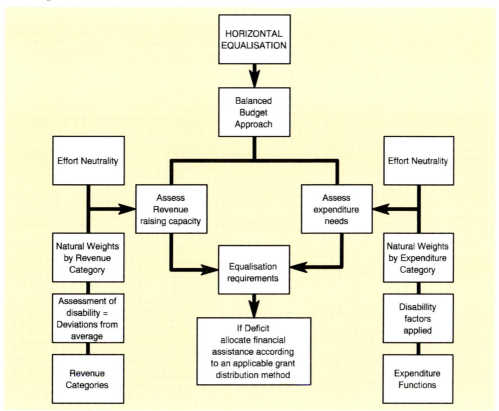

Source: P.A.Cassidy, P. Rao, *Methodology for Financial Assistance Grant Allocations by the Local
Government Grants Commission, Queensland: A Review (Volume 1), April 1993*

Exhibit A7.3
VERTICAL FISCAL IMBALANCE IN AUSTRALIA, 1991-92
The Commonwealth raises more tax than its functions require, whilst the states have more functions
than their revenue can support

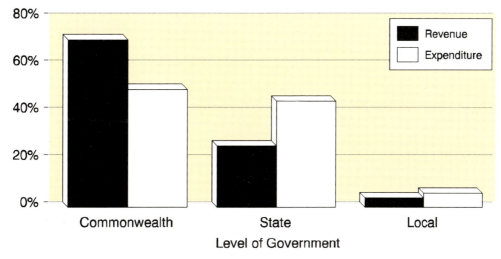

Source: *Financial Relations between the Queensland and Commonwealth Governments,
Queensland State Budget Paper No.7 (1992-93)*

7. The Commonwealth Grants Commission selects criteria for the distribution of grant, which are 'effort neutral' – tries to avoid variables which capture variations in the efficiency of performance by States – and 'policy neutral' – tries to avoid variables which reward or penalise state policy variations. Although the language is dissimilar, these concepts resonate closely with the objectives of the British SSA system, although as British local government has such a confined scope for revenue raising, the revenue capability assumptions in Britain are much simpler.

8. Whilst the British system is one of devising a formula for the sub-division of a predetermined sum, the Australian system attempts to assess the cost drivers of each activity which it is legitimate for states to undertake. Quite a number of considerations survive the criteria of 'effort neutral' and 'policy neutral' and are taken into account in the formulae. Frequently, they have a very marginal effect on the distribution of resources but the inclusion of a burgeoning number of variables makes formulae difficult to comprehend as well as exacerbating the difficulties of data assembly. There is no comprehensive system of 'area cost adjustments' reflecting different levels of employment costs, although Grants Commissions do take into account evidence that service provision faces other unavoidable cost differentials in different locations in Australia.

TENSIONS

9. Australia is not entirely 'at ease' with its grants system. The Commonwealth government is increasingly concerned with the development of 'one Australia' policies which it sees as appropriate in shaping the country to compete in the world economy. It therefore tends to argue for greater policy control over funding to achieve improved performance from Australia plc. General fiscal equalisation grants do not achieve this objective as they empower the states to pursue individual and sometimes diverse policies. Consequently, only a very altruistic Commonwealth government will over-ride the instinct of central government to seek to control the use of its tax resources. Not surprisingly, the States are resistant to any notion that the Commonwealth government should acquire greater policy control over the use of fiscal resources. They argue that fiscal equalisation 'holds the federation together at least from a financial viewpoint. A federal system of government permits both unity and diversity but a federation without equalisation lacks equality. A federal system with fiscal equalisation combines unity, diversity and equality'[1].

10. The Commonwealth government is showing an increasing appetite to develop programmes of action implemented by special purpose payments which are in addition to the general financial assistance grants. Consequently, the Commonwealth is progressively increasing its use of Special Purpose Grants and decreasing the resources made available through general financial assistance grants (Exhibit A7.4). In this tension, one detects echoes of the British/Common Market debate about additionality, with the Commonwealth (EC) not wishing its financial assistance to the States (local government) to be lost in the web of general financial transfers.

11. The States argue that Special Purpose Payments cloud the accountability of each level of government for the provision of public sector services. The Commonwealth government acknowledge this concern but counters with the view that 'As public sector performance assessment and accountability increasingly focuses on outcomes, rather than inputs (such as funds spent or resources used),

---

1   *Queensland State Government, Financial Relations between the Queensland and Commonwealth Governments, Queensland State Budget Paper No.7, 1992-3*

72

Exhibit A7.4
COMPOSITION OF TOTAL COMMONWEALTH PAYMENTS: ALL STATES
The Commonwealth is increasing its use of Special Purpose grants and decreasing its use of general grants

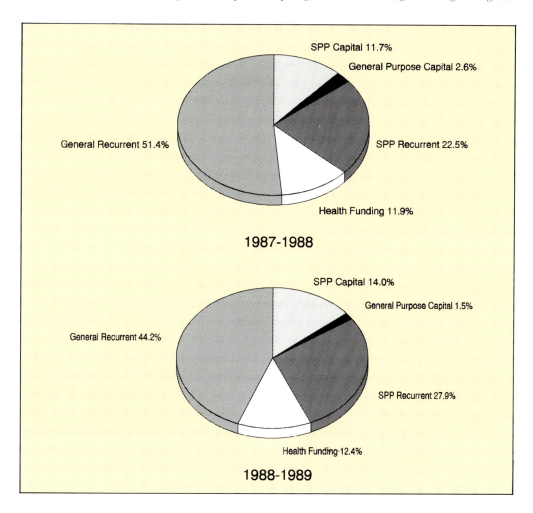

SPP Capital 11.7%

General Purpose Capital 2.6%

General Recurrent 51.4%

SPP Recurrent 22.5%

Health Funding 11.9%

1987-1988

SPP Capital 14.0%

General Purpose Capital 1.5%

General Recurrent 44.2%

SPP Recurrent 27.9%

Health Funding 12.4%

1988-1989

Source: Financial Relations between the Queensland and Commonwealth Governments, Queensland State Budget Paper No.7 (1992-93)

there is greater scope for efficiency improvement and more innovative means of satisfying the Commonwealth's broader policy interests in areas of shared responsibility, while maximising states' autonomy and flexibility in responding to community needs'[1]. The Commonwealth Grants Commission is in the cockpit of the pressures caused by these conflicting perspectives.

12. The Commonwealth Grants Commission interprets its remit to equalise revenue capability amongst the states as obliging it to take into account any special purpose payments when assessing a State's revenue capability. As the Commonwealth Grants Commission uses five year rolling averages, it takes some time for special purpose payments to filter into the assessment system, but the effect of the Commission's 'inclusion' of such payments in its assessment of general

---

1 *Commonwealth financial relations with other levels of government 1992/933, Commonwealth Government Budget Paper No. 4*

fiscal assistance grants is to neutralise the policy focused efforts of the Commonwealth government. States which succeed in obtaining special purpose funds, receive resources early, usually with conditions attached; states which do not attract such funds benefit later from equalising Commonwealth Grants Commission allocations and do not have to meet conditions.

13. The tolerance of the Commonwealth government of this situation can be understood only by reference to the constitutional position which pertains in Australia. But increasingly, funds such as 'Medicare' are being 'quarantined' from the remit of the Commonwealth Grants Commission so that the resource backed differentiating policies of the Commonwealth government have meaningful effect. It is possible that the exclusion of categories of expenditure from the purview of the Commonwealth Grants Commission will engender a 'pack of cards' situation, obliging a comprehensive review of state/commonwealth relations. This problem is not the fault of the Commonwealth Grants Commission – it is a consequence of the historic remit which continues to operate even though political realities have changed.

14. The principles upon which the Commonwealth Grants Commission operates are not without controversy. Their practical effect is to shift resources from the older developed states of Australia (Victoria and New South Wales) to those states such as Western Australia and Northern Territories, where the infrastructure of public services is extending into less developed areas (Exhibit A7.5). The governments of New South Wales and Victoria are increasingly arguing that equity of provision of public services is inimical to the efficiency of the Australian economy i.e. the redistribution of tax revenues through the grants mechanism sends false signals to individuals and companies, leading to sub-optimal location decisions. Similar arguments have been presented at state level to state grants commissions. Not surprisingly, these representations have been countered on the grounds of lack of evidence, by states which would lose grant were the argument to prevail. A recent review by the Industry Commission[1] concludes that 'fiscal equalisation among and within the states provides the capacity to subsidise high cost locations. When grants compensate for high costs, they can effectively compensate for inefficient decision making in urban matters. Any review of Commonwealth Grants Commission matters should address this issue'. Clearly, there is, at least, a case to be answered.

15. The argument between equity and efficiency is one important dimension of a wider issue. In Britain, allegations about political bias in the grants formula have been made. The Department of the Environment defends the SSA as an objective assessment of councils' needs but suspicions that the transparency of data obscures opaque value judgements remain, certainly in the minds of many in local government. In Australia, one might assume that the neutrality of the grants commissions should protect the assessment from distortion, but in practice the value judgements of the people appointed to the relevant commissions become significant. Moreover it is far less obvious what those value judgements are when they lack a political pedigree. All of the Australian Commissions interviewed conceded that they must make judgements in the construction of the basis upon which grants are allocated. In particular, they adjudicate representations and most importantly determine the weights to be attached to variables in the formula. Therefore, whilst using a grants commission system may

---

1   *Industry Commission, Taxation and Financial Policy Impacts on Urban Settlement, December 1992*

Exhibit A7.5
Exhibit A7.5
FINANCIAL ASSISTANCE GRANTS, ALL STATES, DEVIATION FROM AVERAGE 1992-93
The Commonwealth Grants Commission shifts resources from New South Wales and Victoria to other states.

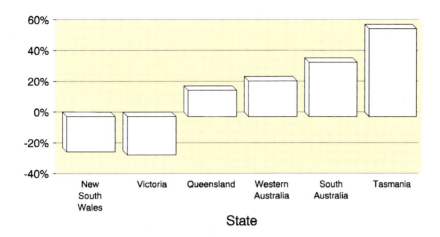

Source: *Financial Relations between the Queensland and Commonwealth Governments, Queensland State Budget Paper No.7 (1992/93)*

remove the suggestion of overt partisan behaviour, it does not remove value judgement. The system possesses strong objective characteristics which clothe a structure of subjective values.

16. In addition, the remit of the Grants Commissions is to a significant degree compromised by the parameters within which they must operate. For good political reasons, the allocation system has been brokered between the various Australian governments to produce a result which does not and cannot achieve equity. For example, insufficient resources are cycled through the process to neutralise the assessment of inequality. Therefore, whilst the Commissions endeavour to equalise the capability of states and of councils within states they can only ameliorate circumstances in the direction of greater equity.

17. Moreover, the sum allocated by the Commonwealth government to state grants commissions for apportionment amongst local councils in states is not allocated on an equitable basis. The Commonwealth distributes the sum to states on a straight per capita basis ignoring disparities between states in terms of needs and resources. Only when it reaches the state grants commissions is it then distributed on a needs/resources formula basis.

18. States' grants formulae have further distortions. Although the formulae would create negative needs for some councils, implying that they should contribute to the equalisation of council resources within a state, negative values are not permitted. Therefore no council can be worse off than a nil beneficiary regardless of the force of the formula.

19. Indeed, the system is distorted even further by a rule that requires 30% of funds made available to each state to be distributed to councils on a per capita basis. Therefore, even well resourced councils attract a platform of grant funding, because of their population. In practice, this protection of the interests of well resourced councils is palatable, because grant support to councils infrequently exceeds 10% of their budgets. Moreover the protection of grant support for well resourced councils in part counteracts the inclination of the needs/resources formula to move resources to the outback.

QUEENSLAND'S SYSTEM

20. The Queensland system (Box A7.B) has proven controversial and the controversy generated understandable debate, of interest to British eyes. The Commonwealth government did not accept the State Grants Commission methodology in 1988/89 and 1989/90, superimposing its own distribution. This has led Queensland to revise and refine its methodology with the assistance of academic consultants.

21. Rates in Queensland are assessed on the basis of unimproved land values. Alone, this

Box A7.B

> The methodology of Queensland involved the creation of a notional 'balanced budget'. 'Its objective requires that provided each local governing body (LGB) uses reasonable effort, the grant to each LGB could ensure that no LGB would function below the average standard of other LGBs in the state'. The amount on the revenue side of the budget is the sum of the assessed revenue capacities of that LGB for each of 5 revenue categories – rates; fees, licences and fines; household garbage and other garbage charges; other charges; interest received. The amount on the expenditure side of the budget is the sum of the assessed expenditure need for that LGB for each expenditure function. The difference between the assessed expenditure need and the assessed revenue capacity – the deficit – is the amount of the equalisation grant e.g. assessed revenue capacity plus equalisation grant equals assessed expenditure need.

would introduce serious distortions as it would fail to capture the resource strength of successful cities and towns. Moreover, as the methodology acknowledges that councils obtain a percentage of their income from fees and charges (much higher in Australia than in the UK, Exhibit A7.6) the equalisation formula needs to acknowledge the differential capability of communities to pay charges. Therefore rates are supplemented in the equalisation formula with data on personal income, which the Australian Census records; urban rates are supplemented by residual retail sales, in the same manner as the gross value of rural production for rural councils.

22. The calculation acknowledges the need to incorporate consideration of 'capital' as well as revenue. The Grants Commission accepted the criticism of its academic consultant that:

> *'The acquisition (creation) of assets and their subsequent replacement at the end of their useful lives is associated with different funding sources and choices and requires a commitment over a longer time-frame than that associated with administration, the operation and maintenance of assets and provision of services. It is suggested that use of recurrent expenditure alone, which includes debts servicing, ignores these differences, and the significance of capital works funding decisions on expenditure needs.'*

Exhibit A7.6
BRISBANE CITY – REVENUE SOURCES
Councils in Austrailia obtain a higher proportion of their income from fees and charges than those in the UK.

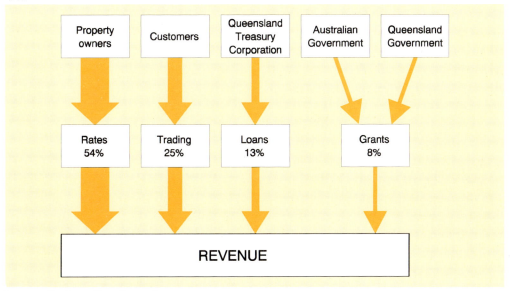

Source: Brisbane City Council

The Grants Commission accepted this advice considering that if only current expenditure were assessed and capital expenditures ignored, bias would be introduced into the assessments.

23. As such, this looks like the capital servicing element of British SSAs. But the consultants would have wished to go further and taken into account the effect of 'asset sales'. They note that 'accounting procedures currently in place in Local Governing Bodies generally (non-accrual accounting) do not presently allow a comprehensive treatment of capital costs incurred by them'. They also recognise that asset sales were often lumpy and therefore difficult to formulate. Nevertheless, these concerns do signal a relevant direction for refinement in Australia, as well as highlighting the absence of accrual accounting and any methodology in Britain to account for the capricious influence of the 'wealth' of councils. SSAs measure current income; they do not differentiate amongst councils' inherited asset wealth.

24. The Queensland study also advocated the use of 5-year rolling averages to avoid the volatility of annual figures. However, these can give rise to some counter-intuitive effects when set alongside the property cycle. As resource capability is probably of greater importance than expenditure needs, the operation of the 5 year rolling average can have the unfortunate consequence of delivering an assessment of resource capability in a recession, based on the property buoyancy of the previous 5 years, and likewise delivering a resource assessment in a boom, based on a previous recession. This interaction between a statistical moving mean and the economic cycle simply illustrates the difficulty in producing credible formulae which lack unintended side effects.

25. Statistical difficulties were also a problem. In some circumstances, Brisbane has an ability to distort the formula because its size makes it hugely dominant in a state of small councils. Any suggestion of regional distribution in Britain would need to take this point into account for we could well end up with a situation of British regions being dominated by their major cities. The

problem of the dominance of lead cities can be overcome with per capita indices but non-linear solutions often emerge. (Exhibit A7.7) The academic consultant to Queensland also pointed out that much of the data failed to meet the criteria of regression and needed to be massaged. Further, differences in accounting practice could interfere with the process. In the first two years of the data series that was examined, Brisbane expended millions of dollars on 'general public services' falling to $100,000 in 1988 and then to zero. The changes arose not because of changes in service level but because of changes in accounting procedures. Brisbane's behaviour caused a major downwards bias in assessed expenditure in this function across the state.

Exhibit A7.7
MAJOR CITIES CAN DOMINATE THE FORMULA
The dominance of major cities can be overcome with per capita indices...

Expenditure (or revenue) $

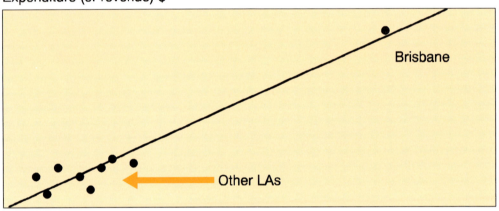

Variable (e.g. Population)

... but non linear solutions often emerge

Expenditure (or revenue) $ per capita

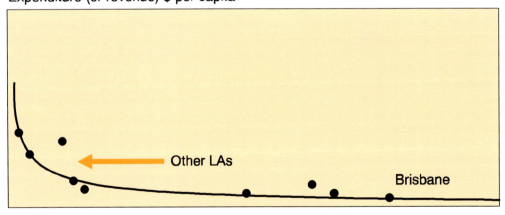

Variable (e.g. Population)

Source: Queensland Local Government Grants Commission Methodology

26. An interesting feature of the system is that it enables one to calculate the amount of grants needed to equalise across the state and compare that figure with the sum available. In Queensland, as in every other Australian state, needs exceed available grant. A final step to distribute grant is thus required. Instead of distributing grant in proportion to the deficit in the notional budget, Queensland distributes it in proportion to the unmet expenditure needs which therefore skews the final distribution in favour of settlements with greater total need rather than greater proportionate need.

27. Interesting features of Queensland are its ability to demonstrate the mismatch between grants and need, its wish to include capital, and the recognition of the relevance of personal income to council funding. Its lessons are in respect of the effect of a large centre on a regional distribution, the difficulties of using annual data without agreed and stable accounting standards and the effect of final arbitrary grant distribution criteria.

THE EMERGING PATTERN

28. Three models are present in the tensions in Australia:-

1.   Equalisation

2.   Special Purpose Payments

3.   Political Brokerage

The equalisation principle is overseen by the Grants Commissions. It is concerned with equalising capability not performance. So states and councils remain free to select their own menu of services. But the Commonwealth government is increasingly concerned that some services be equally available to the consumers across Australia, and in some cases are differentially available to consumers, but on criteria which are set centrally rather than by states. Special Purpose Payments can have conditions attached to them which prescribe outputs. Therefore the Commonwealth government can use them to achieve equivalence of service across states rather than equalisation of capability.

29. A third model is also in existence. If the equalisation model is unacceptable to Commonwealth government because it leaves it muted and ineffectual, and if the Special Purpose Payment system is unacceptable to state government because they lose policy control, a third model of direct political negotiation between states and Commonwealth arises. In the case of post compulsory education described as Technical and Further Education (TAFE) the programme and funding of the service is to be brokered by a round table committee of Commonwealth and states. This explicitly recognises that political interest does not make an easy bedfellow with the independent and neutral distribution of capability by the Grants Commission. Indeed, the underfunding of the equalisation mechanism and the constraining rules which circumscribe the State Grants Commission system provide further evidence of political interference with the operation of an 'expert' grants system.

ASSESSMENT

30. Placing the distribution of grant in the hands of independent grants commissions does not absolve the distribution from value judgements. Subjectivity is still involved – the final test being the acceptability of the result, both to the Commission and other interested parties. In the

case of Australia, the litmus test until recently has broadly been the extent to which the grants system shifts resources from wealthy cities to more remote areas which lack resources. Similarly, resources are moved from the more substantially settled states of Victoria and New South Wales to those states where settlement patterns continue to be extended. In places like Queensland, the formula weighting attributed to variables such as non-English speaking population is low in comparison to the weighting given to the Aboriginal population. If the weightings were reversed money would skew more in the direction of inner city areas with socially disadvantaged populations. In Britain, the opposite pattern is evident. Both systems purport to be objective but produce opposite results. In both cases value judgements are present.

31. In its approach to TAFE, Australia at the Commonwealth level is giving explicit acknowledgement to the importance of political values and will argue these in a political forum with the States. Collective accountability for the consequences will be explicit. Without such explicitness, SSAs and grants commissions obscure accountability for the value judgements which are implicit in their work. There is no shame in having explicit value judgements; accountability would be improved if these were open, explicit and available for public debate.

32. The Australian experience contains a number of other messages for Britain. The first is in the clarity with which the Australians distinguish between vertical fiscal imbalance and horizontal fiscal equalisation. Much of the British argument about the alleged inequalities of SSAs (horizontal fiscal equalisation) may actually be about the inadequacy with which vertical fiscal imbalance is addressed (i.e. that insufficient resources are distributed to enable local needs to be met). Britain could benefit from the Australian vocabulary by better distinguishing what is going on in the distribution of national non-domestic rate and in SSAs in meeting both the resource needs of local government and in equating capability between councils. But before this can be achieved, attention must be given in Britain to the cost drivers of the services which the system supports. The British system of sub-dividing a pre-determined sum without comparison with the costs of services frustrates this possibility.

33. Like the British system, the Australians do not take into account the capital assets of states or councils when equalising capability. In Britain, the ability of some councils to dispose of substantial capital assets has resulted in investment resources which create very low or zero community charge levels. The view is normally taken that such disposals are either good luck or good management and therefore excluded from the SSA system. But in practice some councils enjoy far greater potential to dispose of capital assets than do others, for reasons unconnected with luck or management. The same problem afflicts the Australian system, although with a less convoluted municipal history, the problem is not so severe. However, Australians, like New Zealanders, will in future have the potential to cope with this phenomenon through accrual accounting. By holding asset registers and computing both the asset benefit and the depreciation of assets, the possibility of taking capital induced effects out of the grants system opens up. Britain should accelerate development of accrual accounting not only because of its potential for grants systems, but also because of the improvement in capital asset management which ensues.

34. The clarity with which the Australians define 'standard' is refreshing. In practice, in Britain, standard means average but there has in the past been unhelpful debate about the standard

of service assumed by the SSA system with no-one giving an explicit definition of what standard the consumer should expect. Some readjustment of British terminology would be helpful.

35. The argument in Australia over the inclusion of specific purpose grants is an apt reminder that a lot of resources flow between central and local government in Britain on a basis which is not determined by equity. European resources are a case in point, as is City Challenge and administrative subsidies such as Housing Benefit. This is not to argue that focused funding of this sort is regrettable; to the contrary, but it is an apt reminder that in excluding consideration of such flows, the SSA system fails to achieve a 'pure' equitable system of capability between British councils.

36. The operation of the Australian commissions has burgeoned with ever larger formulae and greater data requirements. This is a problem which Britain avoided, at least to a degree, when GREAs were simplified to SSAs. But in practice, despite efforts in both countries to increase transparency and understandability, the systems seem like 'black boxes' to even well informed observers, leading to exasperation rather than constructive argument.

37. The tensions in Australia between capability and performance are similar to Britain, as is the concern over clarity of accountability when both central and state (local) government provide funding for the same public service. Whilst in Britain, arguments about the tying of grant allocations to their efficient use have entered into debate[1], in Australia no such complications are yet entertained by the Grants Commissions, although some pressure is developing for the system to deliver performance equalisation rather than capacity equalisation. In Britain the obligation on councils to publish performance indicators could reflect central government's expectation of comparability of performance against the equality of capability which SSAs are supposed to provide. A key issue for both countries is the interface between capability and performance. In the Australian case the Commonwealth Grants Commission and State Grants Commissions are declining in importance as Special Purpose Payments increase.

38. Whether one uses the Special Purpose Payment route or the round table brokerage of TAFE, some information on the relationship between capability and performance is necessary. In time, the political process will need carefully framed advice on the effect of funding on performance to inform subsequent allocations. Audit Commission-style studies will assist but the Grants Commission system could receive a new breath of life if its remit was amended to give advice on how to achieve equivalence of performance for the services which are judged nationally important.

39. Similarly in Britain, whilst PIs are a spur to improving performance and achieving greater equivalence in consumer experience, their success is as yet unproven. A reward scheme in which an element of funding follows performance may need to supplement the essential needs-driven model.

---

1   *Remote Control: The Audit Commission has argued that 1% of subsidy supporting Housing Benefit should be distributed on criteria relating to the quality of service*

SUMMARY

40. The lessons from Australia are:-

(a) Independent commissions do not eliminate value judgements – they substitute their own, less obvious values for political values.

(b) The tolerance of a political system for an independent fiscal distribution system has limits, which in Australia are reducing.

(c) Explicit brokerage of political values is possible as in the case of TAFE. This clarifies accountability for decisions.

(d) If a system is left to 'experts', it becomes increasingly sophisticated. Even if the complexity is transparent, interested parties become exasperated with the detail, alleging 'black box' characteristics.

(e) The greater the detail, the more sensitive is the model to fluctuations in data, accounting practices, statistical impurity and economic instability.

(f) Regional distribution systems are at risk of over influence from regional centres.

(g) More detailed attention to assets and to the personal income of the population is possible and practicable.

(h) Like Britain, Australia is becoming increasingly interested in equivalence of performance rather than equivalence of capability.

CONCLUSION

41. The Australian system was examined to assess whether a system of an independent grants commission would add value to the British situation. The answer is that in Australia, it is under pressure. When a system fails to deliver political objectives, its usefulness deteriorates. But political objectives need to be both explicit to facilitate accountability and informed with data to facilitate precision. In Australia, 3 models are evident. If it were decided to set up an independent grants commission in Britain, a way forward might be a combination of their features:

(a) A clear remit from Central Government about the objectives of the grant distribution system. (Australian equivalent – Special Purpose Payments).

(b) The negotiation of that remit with representatives of local authorities. (Australian equivalent – TAFE).

(c) The interpretation of that remit by an independent commission.

By these means accountability for the objectives of the distribution system could be overtly and appropriately political. But the mechanics for the interpretation of that remit could be expert and technical.

A7. Annex

LIST OF ORGANISATIONS VISITED

Councils

Brisbane City Council

Sydney City Council

Bankstown Council

Adelaide City Council

Noarlunga Council

State Governments

Queensland Treasury

New South Wales Department of Local Government

South Australian Treasury

Commonwealth Government

Premier and Cabinet Office, Australian Commonwealth Government

Department of Education

Department of Internal Affairs

Department of Health and Community

Commonwealth Treasury

Grants Commissions

Commonwealth Grants Commission

Queensland State Grants Commission

New South Wales State Grants Commission

South Australian State Grants Commission

Other Organisations

New South Wales Auditor General

Australian Local Government Association

Queensland Local Government Commission

Alan Morton – Independent Consultant

Appendix 8

MORE THAN YOU WANTED TO KNOW?
AN INDEX OF BACKGROUND PAPERS PREPARED FOR
THE STUDY WHICH ARE AVAILABLE ON REQUEST.

Below is a numbered list of papers prepared for the study. A set is available from the Audit Commission at £15.00 net, plus postage and packing.

8.1 The Relationship between Local Authority Budgets, Activities and Standard Spending Assessments (SSAs)

Summary of Paper by KPMG Management Consulting

8.2 The Impact of SSAs on Local Authority Budgets

Paper by Peter Smith, University of York

8.3 Review of the Capital Financing SSA

Paper by Price Waterhouse Management Consultants

8.4 Fire and Highway Maintenance SSAs

Paper by Stephen Lord

8.5 Variations on a Theme – a Comparison of SSAs with Allocation Systems in Europe

Paper by Glen Bramley, School of Advanced Urban Studies, Bristol

8.6 A Review of SSAs in Wales

Paper by Paul Smith, Audit Commission

8.7 Review of Grant Aided Expenditure (GAE) in Scotland: A Comparison with the English SSA System

Paper by Paul Smith, Audit Commission

8.8 Analysis of Results of the Audit Commission Survey of Local Authority Views of the SSA System.

Paper by Paul Smith, Audit Commission

8.9 Standard Spending Assessments – Regression Formulae Analysis

Paper by Bhupinder Jatana, University of Surrey.

90 0388762 X

WITHDRAWN
FROM
UNIVERSITY OF PLYMOUTH
LIBRARY SERVICES

Passing the Bucks:

Appendices

Volume 2

LONDON: HMSO

UNIVERSITY OF PLYMOUTH

Item No.	900 388762 X
Date	2 0 MAY 1999 Z
Class No.	336.014 AUD
Contl. No.	011 8860801

LIBRARY SERVICES

© Crown copyright 1993

Applications for reproduction should be made to HMSO

Printed in the UK for the Audit Commission at Press on Printers
ISBN 011 886 080 1

London : HMSO

Audit Commission, Local Government Report No.5 (Appendices), 1993